Cambridge English Readers

Level 6

Series editor: Phi

D0401754

Deadly Harvest

Carolyn Walker

CAMBRIDGE
UNIVERSITY PRESS

CAMBRIDGE
UNIVERSITY PRESS

University Printing House, Cambridge CB2 8BS, United Kingdom

Cambridge University Press is part of the University of Cambridge.

It furthers the University's mission by disseminating knowledge in the pursuit of education, learning and research at the highest international levels of excellence.

www.cambridge.org
Information on this title: www.cambridge.org/9780521776974

© Cambridge University Press 1999

This publication is in copyright. Subject to statutory exception and to the provisions of relevant collective licensing agreements, no reproduction of any part may take place without the written permission of Cambridge University Press.

First published 1999
Reprinted 2016

Printed in the United Kingdom by Hobbs the Printers Ltd

A catalogue record for this publication is available from the British Library

ISBN 978-0-521-77697-4 Paperback

Cambridge University Press has no responsibility for the persistence or accuracy of URLs for external or third-party internet websites referred to in this publication, and does not guarantee that any content on such websites is, or will remain, accurate or appropriate. Information regarding prices, travel timetables and other factual information given in this work is correct at the time of first printing but Cambridge University Press does not guarantee the accuracy of such information thereafter.

Contents

Characters

Superintendent George Ferguson: head of the South-West Police Force.

Detective Chief Inspector (DCI) Jane Honeywell: the new head of Criminal Investigation Department (CID).

Detective Inspector (DI) Pete Fish.

Detective Sergeant (DS) Penny Kingdom.

Detective Constable (DC) Tony Reilly.

Detective Constable (DC) Maggie Pincombe.

Police Constable (PC) Dick Plumb.

Woman Police Constable (WPC) Morgan.

Mervin Peck: a sheep farmer.

Jack Peck: Mervin's brother, a scientific director at Hunter Products.

Jo Keane: the managing director at Hunter Products.

Brian Millman: a farmhand on Chittleham Farm.

Susan Peck: Jack Peck's wife.

Rose Carter: a part time teacher and statistician.

Elisa Scott: a member of PAW.

Pat James: a police pathologist.

Dr Fahid: a doctor at Pilton hospital.

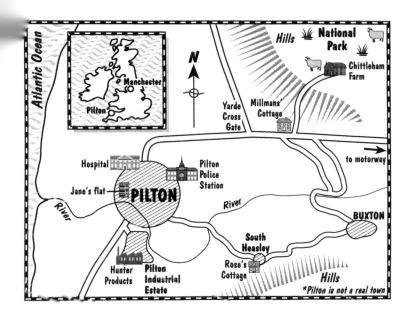

Acronyms

PAW: Project for Animal Welfare
RSPCA: Royal Society for the Prevention of Cruelty to Animals
ID: Official Identification (of a person)
DNA: (deoxyribonucleic acid) used for genetic fingerprinting
MI6: a branch of the British Secret Service

Prologue

'Ah!' she cried and sat down on the wet grass, breathing heavily. The sudden, sharp pain had been so surprising that she couldn't imagine what had caused it. Then she saw, attached still to the back of her hand, a bee delivering its poison into her skin. Horrified, she knocked it away and watched the redness and swelling begin while the pain intensified . . .

She heard footsteps, rubber boots kicking small stones from the path so that they rolled down the hill. Looking up, she saw the face, black as thunder.

'Hey, you! Push off!'

From deep within her came a strange, bitter laugh that she couldn't control. 'I know what's going on,' she said, breathing heavily. 'I'm going to the police.'

Her fingers found the handle of something, an axe, leaning against the wall. She picked it up.

She stood up, took a few steps back on the stony path and raised the axe in front of her. She couldn't look at that face boiling with anger. She concentrated on the black boots, but these moved quickly out of view. Hands grabbed the axe. She watched with a strange interest as it swung away from her, out of her hands, and then back towards her. She noticed how this monstrous-looking face seemed hypnotised now, a robot, programmed and unable to stop what was about to happen. Her eyes closed just before she heard a distant thud, and a terrible, blinding pain exploded inside her head.

Chapter 1   *Going south*

It was early spring and the sun was pouring through the window of a small flat on the first floor of an elegant three-storey house. Out of the window a pair of swans could be seen flying over the river which passed through the west-country market town of Pilton. A woman, Jane Honeywell, stood at the window watching the swans' flight, dressed in her night-clothes. A few days ago, from her flat in the middle of Manchester, she had seen the sun rise between the rows of smoke-blackened redbrick houses, up into the polluted city sky. Here the sunlight was dancing on the water and the air was clean.

Pilton was a small town of some 20,000 inhabitants in the south-west of England. There were a few factories which made things like clothes, shoes, chemicals and electrical parts but, more importantly, Pilton was a market town where the farmers from the surrounding areas brought their cows and sheep to sell every Thursday. However, these days there was not much money in farming, especially on the small lonely hill farms.

Fortunately for the local economy Pilton was a popular part of the world for holidays. In the summer, thousands of people would bring their money and their families to the local beaches and villages, which, with their old cottages and pretty gardens, seemed to belong to times past. Compared to the cities of the north and centre of the country, here it was peaceful and quiet and beautiful. The visitors would return home and dream of escaping to a rural life of changing seasons, of digging the soil, planting and harvesting.

At the moment, though, the woman was missing Alan, her ex-boyfriend, and his morning cheerfulness. What was he doing right now? She could feel his absence in the weight of the silence around her. She wondered how long it would take before her new environment would no longer feel like a foreign country. Professionally, she had done the right thing, there was no question about that. But the memory of Alan's expressionless face as she had packed her suitcases filled her with a sharp sadness.

'You're mad, Jane darling,' her mother had complained. 'Why don't you just marry him, have some kids and settle down like everyone else?'

'My cat's quite enough for me at the moment,' she had joked, curiously unable to explain to her long-suffering mother that the relationship was going nowhere, that she enjoyed her work too much to give it up for domesticity. Anyway, Alan had refused to leave his own work and go with her. So that was that.

Suddenly she became aware of a loud hissing sound and she looked round, alarmed. The milk for her coffee had boiled over and there was a steaming pool of sticky white liquid on the cooker. She swore loudly, simultaneously noticing the time. It was nearly 8.15 a.m.

'Oh, my God, I'm going to be late! Help! Julian, you useless animal, where are my tights?' Jane addressed this question to her cat, which was asleep on a chair by the window. Julian the cat was disgusted by his new home and had already fought with the large black cat next door.

Working fast, Jane picked up a piece of toast and held it in her teeth. She rescued what was left of the milk and poured it into a mug. She looked briefly at the burnt mess on the cooker: she would clean it up later. With one hand she drank the mud-coloured coffee and ate her toast while with the other she searched through several open suitcases on the floor, trying to find a pair of tights.

'Julian, I must get organised,' she told the cat, as piles of clothes fell out onto the floor. Julian took no notice.

In fifteen minutes she was ready. She locked up the flat and went rapidly down the stairs. Outside it was chilly despite the spring sun. There was a strong wind coming in off the sea from the south-west and she wished she had managed to find her winter coat.

When she finally spotted her silver-grey Mazda sports car, which she had left in a public car park round the corner, she was unpleasantly surprised to see that around the door handle there were scratch marks and the door was unlocked. Someone had clearly forced it open.

'Oh no, I don't believe it! The bastards!' she groaned. Inside the car, there was a black hole near the steering wheel and some wires were hanging loose from where the radio cassette player had once been.

'I thought I'd left this kind of thing behind. Obviously not,' she muttered angrily, getting in and starting the engine.

It took her more than twenty minutes to drive the four kilometres to her new place of work: the town in which she had come to live apparently had serious traffic problems.

She sat in the long queue of cars, nose to tail as they approached a roundabout, and a wave of nerves began in her stomach, made worse by the fact that she knew she would have to watch out for what her former boss had termed the 'dinosaurs', the people to whom a woman in a senior management position was a foreign, unwelcome creature. The dinosaurs would be watching every move she made and would lose no time in putting her to the test.

Arriving finally at her destination she glanced at her watch: it was almost 9.00. Hurriedly she parked her car and then walked as calmly as she could manage up to the main entrance to the dull grey stone building that was Pilton Police Station. She pushed her hair back out of her eyes, pulled her jacket down and opened the door.

'Well, here goes. Good luck,' Jane Honeywell said to herself as she stepped inside.

Chapter 2 *Nothing exciting ever happens*

'Good morning, madam, can I help you?' said the police constable at the reception desk, looking at Jane carefully. Who was this woman? He did not remember having seen her before. She was tall and her face was pretty with short dark hair neatly cut. The sharp lines of her dark suit, together with the white silk blouse and low-heeled black shoes, gave her a businesslike appearance. Was she a lawyer, new to the area, come to visit one of the bad boys arrested in the night for stealing a car? The policeman guessed, accurately, that she was in her early thirties.

'Good morning, Constable. Yes,' Jane said, holding up an identification card, 'I'm Detective Chief Inspector Jane Honeywell and, as I expect you know, I'm beginning work here today as head of the Criminal Investigation Department. And your name is . . . ?'

'Oh, er . . . yes, ma'am. I'm Police Constable Dick Plumb, ma'am.' PC Plumb stammered, looking confused. He had heard a rumour that the new head of CID was going to be a woman but, as he had not taken it all that seriously, he had forgotten about it.

'What's the matter, Constable Plumb? Is there a problem?' Jane thought she knew what the problem was. 'Have you never seen a DCI wearing a skirt before?'

'Yes . . . er . . . no, ma'am. No problem, no problem at all,' said Constable Plumb hurriedly.

'In that case,' Jane said, 'do you think you could tell the Superintendent that I'm here, please?'

'Yes, ma'am, of course,' said PC Plumb. 'If you'd like to go through that door and sit down, I'll ask him to come down.'

Unsure whether to open the door for her – maybe she wouldn't like it – he remained behind his desk and picked up the internal phone. 'Strange that PC Plumb didn't seem to be expecting me,' she reflected as she waited. 'Didn't they communicate with each other properly in this place?'

All things considered, Jane Honeywell was glad she had come here. It had all happened very quickly. She had seen the DCI job in Pilton advertised: a new type of place from what she was used to, but it would be useful experience, especially if she wanted to reach the very top. Her boss had encouraged her to go for the necessary promotion, even though she was perhaps a little too young to be a Detective Chief Inspector.

'Come on, Jane,' he had persuaded her. 'We need some more bright women at the top in the police force and you've got what it takes, I know it. And the boys respect you.'

'Oh yeah? Ha ha.' She had been doubtful.

'Go on, they'll love you. Go for it!'

Unconvinced, she nevertheless prepared for the interview, discovering that the area for which Pilton Police Station served as the Divisional Headquarters was huge, as it included the surrounding countryside and several other market towns besides Pilton. Much of the police work, she guessed, would probably involve a lot of time driving from village to village.

Afterwards she had joked with Superintendent George Ferguson, the Pilton Divisional Head. 'No doubt the guys make sure they go past a nice country pub in the middle of nowhere at lunchtime!'

'Oh yes,' George had agreed with a smile, clearly liking her blunt sense of humour. 'They can certainly fill up the hours doing very little, if they put their minds to it!'

Then, to her surprise, her promotion had gone through and she had been offered the Pilton job. And now, finally, here she was, in a place, she imagined, which was light years away from the northern city ways with which she had grown up.

'Hello, there!' A tall, grey-haired man in his fifties appeared at the foot of a flight of stairs and held out a hand. 'Welcome to Pilton, Jane.'

'Thank you, sir,' Jane replied with a smile, giving George Ferguson's hand a firm shake.

'Come on then, come and meet the gang. I'll show you round and then leave you to get settled. You'll find several reports on your desk waiting for your attention.'

They set off up the stairs and George opened the door into a room full of computers and strange faces – mostly, though not quite all, male. Everyone stopped work and turned to look at Jane as she came in. All of a sudden the room was quiet except for the sound of the computers.

'I'd like you all to meet DCI Jane Honeywell,' George announced. 'As you know, she will be taking over the running of this department as from today.'

'Good morning, everyone,' Jane addressed her new colleagues. 'Well, I'm delighted to be here. I hope we'll all get along together. As the day goes on, I'll be talking to

13

each of you. I'm a hands-on kind of manager so I don't stay in my office with the door always closed.'

There was silence, and nobody moved. After a short pause, a woman's voice murmured, 'Nice to meet you, ma'am, welcome to Pilton.' From somewhere in the room, Jane could just hear a soft laugh. She thought she caught the words 'Hands on what?', though she could not be sure.

'All right,' she smiled. 'I'll be seeing you all later.' As she and George went out, behind her several people started talking at once.

'They're a good crowd really,' Superintendent Ferguson told her. 'Don't take them too seriously.'

'No, sir,' said Jane. 'I won't.'

'Once they see they can trust you, you'll have no trouble,' George continued. 'You've come to us from a big city but life moves slowly down here. People are used to the way things are and they don't like change, as I'm sure you'll appreciate.'

After a tour of the building, they were back where they had started, in the corridor outside the CID office, which could be observed through some internal windows. Some of the occupants had noticed her presence and stared unsmiling as she and George went into her new office.

'Well, this is where you'll be,' George said. 'I'll come back a little later and we'll go through a few bits and pieces. I expect you'll find we do things differently down here.'

George disappeared and, with a sense of relief, Jane sat down at her desk. She was still in a sweat from having to hurry to arrive on time. She needed to try to relax.

She turned and looked behind her through the external windows. Beyond the houses there were rolling hills and green fields, and between the hills and the town, the river wound its way out to the Atlantic Ocean, only a few kilometres in the distance. Away from the coast, the land rose sharply up to the hills which formed a national park. Here sheep fed on the rough grass of open moorland and hill farmers worked hard for a living.

'Could be worse, I suppose,' she said to herself.

She had just begun to read through a long report on the recent wave of small crimes when she was interrupted by a knock at the door and a young woman in her twenties came in with a tray of coffee. Jane remembered her face from the CID office.

'Hello,' she said. 'You are . . . ?'

'Detective Constable Maggie Pincombe, ma'am.'

'Pleased to meet you, Maggie.' Jane smiled. Then, after a moment, she asked, 'Just out of interest, how many women are there in this station?'

'Well,' Maggie thought for a moment. 'Let me see. Not many really. There's one or two new constables who have just started on the beat, which makes half a dozen there, plus a few in Traffic. Only men in Special Operations and Dogs. But there's me and Detective Sergeant Penny Kingdom in CID,' she finished cheerfully.

'Oh,' said Jane, 'was that Penny I saw over by the window in the office talking to someone?'

'Yes, that was her,' said Maggie. 'With DI Pete Fish. He's been in charge till you got here. He applied for promotion to DCI, you know. Didn't get it, though.'

'Really?' Jane said.

'Yes,' Maggie went on. 'If you can get Pete Fish on your side, you won't have any trouble.'

'Thanks for the tip.' Jane smiled, with more confidence than she felt. 'Oh Maggie, I've just remembered. Someone broke into my car last night and stole my radio cassette player. I'll need an incident report form.'

'Oh no, that's bad luck.' Maggie was sympathetic. 'There's a lot of car crime round here. It's been on the increase for the last six months.'

'So I see from this report,' Jane said.

'That's what we spend most of our time on,' Maggie told her. 'Plus the occasional house break-in. Nothing *really* exciting ever happens.'

*   *   *

Later, back in her flat, Jane stared hopelessly at the chaos on the floor in the sitting room: she was too exhausted to do anything about it tonight. She picked up a cloth and started to rub at the burnt milk on the cooker.

What if she had made a dreadful mistake? Would she really be able to win the trust of her new colleagues? Should she just pick up her suitcases and go back to Manchester?

Just then the phone rang.

'Hello, love. Well, how was your first day? Did you get on all right?' The northern accent was unmistakable.

'Oh hello, Mum,' Jane said, weakly. 'Yes, thanks, fine. Everything's fine.' It was comforting, after all, to talk to a familiar voice.

After speaking to her mother for a while, she felt more cheerful. Tomorrow was another day and she had to continue her chats with each of the members of her team. Especially Pete Fish, who had somehow managed to avoid her today.

Chapter 3 *Time to wake up*

A week later, on Monday evening at about 11 p.m., Jane was sitting in her flat, a glass of wine in her hand, and Julian the cat curled up on the sofa next to her. The suitcases had gone from the sitting room and were piled in her bedroom, and most, though not quite all, of their contents were now in cupboards and drawers.

It had been the first flat she had looked at when she had come down for her interview and she had liked it immediately because of its river view. Unfortunately, she had been in such a rush that she had not really noticed that the yellow flowery wallpaper was not to her taste. Never mind, redecorating would give her something to do outside work.

Work. It had become clear after a few days that the department needed a shake-up. Unlike Manchester, where the police force struggled hard to contain violent crimes and drug-related offences, her new colleagues seemed to take a more relaxed approach. When she enquired about the steadily increasing number of car thefts and house break-ins, Jane was informed that these crimes were probably being carried out by just one or two people – most likely in-comers to the area from the north, they had said pointedly.

'You know it's five per cent of the population that commits ninety-five per cent of the crime?' DC Tony

Reilly told her. 'Well, round here it's one per cent. It's just a matter of working through the usual suspects. Easy!'

Despite the apparent simplicity of the action needed, the crimes had remained unsolved for too long, Jane thought. So, while mindful of George Ferguson's warning about making changes, she decided that her department needed to try a different approach.

Earlier today she had asked Detective Inspector Pete Fish to come into her office. She knew she ought to discuss her ideas with him, despite the fact that, in their first meeting, he had not been especially communicative.

'Yes, *ma'am*, what can I do for you?' he had asked this morning, as he leant against the door of her office, a large man with broad shoulders and a slightly overweight stomach. He said *ma'am* in an American accent for a joke, and he was grinning in a way that was annoying. He had looked pleased with himself, as if he knew something that she didn't.

Just then the phone by her elbow rang, bringing her back to the present. 'Yes?' she said.

'Sorry to disturb you, ma'am,' said a voice she thought was PC Plumb, 'but a body has been found.'

'What? Good grief! Who said nothing ever happened around here? OK, I'm on my way. Give me the details.' Jane felt herself switching into a familiar routine, one that she had imagined she would not have to use very often in this rural location.

'It's at Chittleham Farm, up on the moor. You take the main road out of Pilton and first left after Yarde Gate Cross. If you've got a map, you'll see it,' PC Plumb told her.

18

'Don't worry, I'll find it. Tell the rest of them to get out there, will you?'

'The Fi . . . I mean . . . DI Fish is already out there. He was on duty this evening. He said to call you.'

Nice of him, Jane thought. She could just imagine his grinning face.

Outside, the usual south-west wind was whistling through the quiet streets and rain hammered on the roofs of the houses and parked cars. Jane found her car and, with her map open on the seat next to her, she set off a little anxiously for the moor. She would not have chosen this particular night to go driving around in the dark in an unknown part of the countryside.

While she tried to concentrate on the task of finding her way, her thoughts kept slipping back to her earlier conversation with Pete Fish.

'OK, Pete,' she had said. 'Come in and shut the door.' Standing in front of her desk, she had noticed that she was as tall as he was.

'All these stolen cars,' she had begun, looking him straight in the eyes. 'We really should do something about them.'

'I think we're doing all we can, ma'am,' Pete Fish replied. He stopped talking in his American accent and yawned slightly.

'I'm afraid I don't agree, Pete,' Jane told him bluntly. 'Let's see. What do you usually do? You find someone who you know has committed one of the crimes. Then you persuade him to admit that he has done another fifteen similar jobs. Which is fine. It makes life easy for everyone.

But then how do you explain the fact that the rate for these crimes is increasing?'

'Well,' Pete Fish explained, 'the word on the street is that it's criminals from up north. They come in on our nice new motorway, take a car and drive it out of the area as fast as they can. Then it goes onto the national computer and there's nothing more for us to do.'

'Oh come on, that's pathetic. Do you just sit here and wait for it happen?' Jane said. 'How about setting up a few road checkpoints? Or some observation posts?'

'There are not enough people to do all that,' Pete said.

'And why not?'

'Well,' Pete said, 'as you'll know, we've got a "zero tolerance" scheme on street crime operating at the moment. All the drunks, thieves and undesirables that get arrested . . . well, they have to be transported to prison, to court . . . That uses up a lot of vehicles and staff.'

'Zero tolerance schemes don't work,' Jane pointed out. 'The bad guys just move elsewhere.'

'Possibly.' Pete's reply had been short, almost rude.

'Let's get things straight right from the beginning, Pete,' Jane had said, realising that she had to get tough. 'You may not like the fact that I'm your boss, but I'm here to stay, so you'll have to get used to it. I'll discuss zero tolerance with Superintendent Ferguson. In the meantime, I'm going to draw up plans for a major crack-down on car crime and burglaries. It seems to me that life is a bit quiet round here. In fact, it's so quiet I think you're all asleep. Well, it's time to wake up now.'

'Yes, ma'am.' Pete had not looked happy. 'But quite honestly, I think it'll be a waste of time.'

'Well, I'll be the judge of that, thank you.' Jane turned away to continue working.

Pete went out, shutting the door loudly. Jane could see through the internal windows that he was talking to some of the other men in the CID office. From time to time they looked towards her room, laughing.

Now, thinking about this incident as she was driving along in the dark and the rain, Jane would have preferred not to have to face Pete and the others tonight. She had not particularly wanted to come into conflict with the men she would have to work with so soon after starting her job. And now there was a serious crime to deal with, she could not afford to make any mistakes.

Oh hell! Was that Yarde Cross Gate? She would have to walk back to the signpost. She stopped the car and, taking a torch, walked back to where she thought she had seen a signpost. She reached the crossroads and found that the signpost no longer gave any useful information: one arm had fallen off and the other pointed back to where she had come from. Annoyed, she went back to her car and studied her map, though she could make no sense of it. She would just have to carry on until there was another sign. About three kilometres further on there was a left turn, and a small house on the corner where there was a light in an upstairs window. She decided to knock at the door.

'I'm sorry to bother you,' she said to the elderly man who looked nervously round the half-open door. 'But I'm looking for Chittleham Farm.' She showed him her police identity card.

He looked carefully at it, seemed satisfied, and mumbled something in a strong local accent. But with the high wind and his strange accent, Jane could hardly make out what he was saying. She understood, however, that she was going in the right direction.

'Thanks. I'm sorry to have got you out of bed,' she said and set off again.

To her relief, the old man was right. After a couple of minutes there were blue flashing lights ahead, and drawing nearer, she could see several police cars, their yellow stripes glowing in the dark. A black and white sheepdog appeared barking loudly as she drove down a narrow lane leading to a large farmhouse. She parked and walked towards a uniformed officer, behind whom a group of people were talking excitedly. One of the figures moved away from the group and approached her. It was Detective Inspector Pete Fish.

Chapter 4   *Not a pretty sight*

'Evening, ma'am. Nice night to be out, isn't it?' Pete remarked. 'Got your boots on? It's a bit wet.'

'Don't worry, I'll be all right.' She followed Pete into a field and they climbed a slight hill. The wind and rain and wet grass at her feet were cold. She held her coat tight around her and shivered.

'You found the place all right, then?' Pete asked pleasantly, making conversation.

'Oh yes, no problem. I knocked at a house a mile or two back and woke up an old man. Couldn't understand a word he said but I got the general idea,' Jane replied, equally polite. 'The local accent's strong, isn't it?'

'You'll get used to it.' Pete was obviously smiling in the dark.

They approached a large tent at the top of the hill. The tent was brightly lit by powerful lamps and they could see shadows of people moving around the scene of the crime. Pete gave Jane some plastic slippers to put over her shoes and they went into the tent and through a circle of red tape.

Inside, several Scene-of-Crime Officers (SOCOs), dressed in white coverall suits, were moving around an old pick-up truck, busily collecting fingerprints, filming the scene with a video camera, and looking with great care through the covered area for hairs, fibres, blood, anything which might provide vital clues.

Pete introduced Jane to a woman holding a torch. 'This is Dr Pat James, the pathologist.'

'How do you do?' Jane said, shaking hands, vaguely aware that she was pleased to find another woman in a largely male world.

'Want to have a look? It's not a pretty sight,' Pat James said, pointing her powerful torch into the back of the pick-up truck where a woman in her early forties lay on her back as if she had just fallen asleep. Behind the woman's head some bags of animal feed were piled on top of each other, half-covered by a rubber sheet. She was wearing boots, thick trousers and a heavy jacket, as if she had been out walking, perhaps across the moor. In death, her face had collapsed inwards like a balloon from which the air had escaped, but there was not much blood – just some on the top of her head, where someone had made an ugly wound and probably broken her skull.

'Who is she?' Jane turned to Pete.

'Rose Carter. From South Heasley. That's a village just outside Pilton,' he explained. 'We got an ID from the cards in her wallet.'

'So who found her?' Jane asked.

'A local lad, apparently,' Pete answered. 'Brian Millman. He helps the farmer during lambing time. As I expect you know, lambs are born at all times of the day or night and the sheep have to be checked regularly.'

'Thank you for that explanation,' Jane murmured.

'Not at all. Anyway, Brian's a bit simple, according to the farmer. The farmer's Mervin Peck, by the way. He farms the place on his own, apart from the help that Brian gives him. Look at that . . .' Pete pointed at a large wooden box on the ground close to the pick-up.

But Jane had already started to walk towards the box, which had legs and a sloping roof. 'What is it?' she asked.

'Er . . . it's a beehive,' Pete said, with some amusement. 'Haven't you ever seen one before?'

'Not like that,' Jane said sharply. 'What's it doing there?'

'It was on top of the rubber sheet that covered the body,' Pete replied. He grinned with boyish enthusiasm. 'It's like something out of a detective novel. "The beekeeper murderer". You know, the murderer's "signature". . .'

'Well, perhaps,' Jane replied, a little stiffly. 'More likely the beehive was the nearest heavy object to hold the sheet down. It's very windy, you know. Come on, we need to talk to the farmer and this boy.'

In the farmhouse kitchen, the farmer, Mervin Peck, was sitting in a brown armchair that was so old the insides were falling out. Two uniformed police constables were standing with their backs to a large, old-fashioned cooker. A young man of around seventeen or eighteen was seated on a wooden chair, resting an elbow on a big square table on which stood several empty mugs, half a bottle of milk and a bag of sugar. Nobody was speaking.

Although it was warm enough inside, the impression was of a house given the minimum of attention. There were no curtains at the windows, and the ancient, worn carpet was caked with mud. Spiders' webs hung in dark corners. The once-white walls and ceiling were dusty and yellow with the stain of tobacco smoke. Obviously the needs of the farm and its animals came before those of housework and home decoration.

'Good evening, sir,' Jane said to the farmer. 'I'm DCI Jane Honeywell. I'm afraid we have to ask you a few questions.'

'Yes,' said Mervin Peck in a dull voice. 'Go ahead.'

'Well, can you tell us what happened, please?' she asked quietly.

'I was asleep,' Mervin began, as if he was unaccustomed to speaking. 'Gone to bed early. Lambing time, see? Next thing I know is the boy there, Brian, he's pulling at me, shouting some nonsense about the police. Couldn't understand what he was on about. Anyway, I had to get up, go outside with him. Took me up into the field with the truck in.'

'It *is* your pick-up truck, then, sir?' Pete interrupted. 'Is that where you normally keep it?'

'Often leave it in the field overnight if it's got feed in the back. Saves time in the morning.'

'What time was this?' Jane asked.

'About 9.30. Couldn't understand what he wanted so I started to shout at him. He's not quite all there, you know. Never know what he'll do next sometimes.' Mervin touched the side of his head with his forefinger. 'We got to the pick-up and he pointed at the back. At the beehive. First I thought he just wanted to show me the beehive and I thought, terrific, wakes me up just for this. Then I realised he wanted me to look under the sheet. Pulled it back and there was a pair of feet sticking out. I tell you, it gave me a fright. Ain't never seen a dead body before. I mean, I seen plenty of dead animals, but not a human being. Tried pushing the feet, just in case it was an old tramp or someone, having a sleep. But they didn't move. They looked like a woman's feet, quite small, you know, neat-looking.

'Anyway, Brian said he'd wanted another bucket and came out here to get one from the pick-up. I said we'd better get the police and he said could he dial 999, like they do on TV.'

'Did you have a look at the woman's face?' Jane asked him. 'You're right, it is a woman.'

'No. Didn't want to,' Mervin said flatly.

'Do you have any idea who she might be?'

'None at all,' he replied. 'Don't know who she is or how she got there. There's only me lives here and no-one comes up here except Brian and my brother. He keeps his bees out in one of the fields.'

'Her name's Rose Carter,' Pete said.

'Never heard of her,' said Mervin.

'Will I be on TV?' asked Brian.

'Maybe, son. You did well,' Pete told him. 'Well done.' Brian looked pleased.

'Did you see anyone here today, Brian?' Jane asked.

'Yes, I saw Mr Peck.' Brian seemed surprised by the question.

'No, I mean, anyone else?' Jane said. Brian seemed to become suddenly shy. He looked at the floor.

'What time did you come to work today, Brian?' Jane tried again. Brian looked at Mervin.

'He's no good at telling the time,' Mervin explained. 'He starts work at about five in the afternoon. Does 5 p.m. to 5 a.m. Lives just up the road with his grandfather, old Mr

27

Millman.' He must have been the old man I spoke to, Jane thought.

Outside a vehicle could be heard arriving. Jane stood up and went out of the house to watch the body, now contained in a body bag, being loaded into the back of the undertaker's car and taken away to the mortuary for a post-mortem.

From behind her Pete murmured, 'Well, this is your first major incident, ma'am.'

'I'm aware of that, thank you, Fish,' Jane said sharply. 'I want an incident room set up immediately, with everyone in the department involved. We may need to call in some help from the other departments. I want everyone there at 8 a.m. On the dot.'

Chapter 5   *The investigation begins*

The next morning, the CID office was electric with excitement. When Jane arrived just before 8 a.m., people were gathered together in small groups, or else rushing around with pieces of paper and answering endlessly ringing phones. You'd think there had never been a good murder before, Jane thought to herself as Pete walked in through the open office door.

'Good morning, ma'am,' he said, all smiles despite his rather tired appearance. He needed a shave and there were dark shadows below his eyes.

'I'd appreciate it if you would knock before you come in, Pete,' Jane said. 'Even if you have been up all night.'

'Sorry, ma'am,' he said. 'Can you come into CID now? We've had to book a news conference for 9.30 as the local media have somehow got hold of the story already.'

'OK, we'll talk to the team first, then I'll deal with the press,' Jane said. 'Let's go.'

In the crowded CID office, people had found seats wherever they could, on chairs and tables. Everyone watched Jane expectantly as she walked over to a large whiteboard at one end of the untidy room.

'Talk us through what we've got so far, will you, Pete?' she instructed him.

'OK, well, besides the ID on the body, not a lot as yet. The postmortem results should be in around midday. Mr

Peck says he left his pick-up in the field at about 4.30 p.m. yesterday, before the lad arrived. And he gave us his brother's name and address: a Mr Jack Peck. Lives at 23 Ilford Terrace, Pilton. Married, no children. Works at Hunter Products in Pilton.'

'What about the SOCOs? They get anything?' Detective Sergeant Penny Kingdom spoke up.

'Some fingerprints off the pick-up truck and the beehive, which they're running a computer check on now,' Pete said. 'Plus quite a lot of bits and pieces we can run DNA checks on.'

'Right, then,' Jane said. 'We need to get as much background as we can. Did Rose Carter work? Who were her friends? What do the neighbours know about her? When was the last time she was seen and where? What was she doing before she died and why? You know the stuff, I hope.'

Jane watched as Pete wrote on the whiteboard all the questions that she had just listed. 'Just so we don't forget anything,' he said. She looked at him with raised eyebrows. 'It's a while since any of us have had to do this, you know,' he said, defensively.

'Mm, I can see that,' Jane said. 'Anyway, when I've spoken to the journalists, I'm off to Chittleham Farm again. I'd like to look around in daylight.'

'Shall I come along too?' Pete asked.

'No. I'd like you to stay and look after things here,' Jane replied. Didn't he think she could handle Mr Peck, or what?

'Would you like a driver, just in case?'

'In case what? Oh all right, I suppose I *might* get lost in the depths of the countryside and you might never see me again,' Jane said acidly. In fact, it would probably be quicker to have someone with her who knew the way. 'Tony, you come with me, please.'

'Don't forget your boots,' Pete added with a grin. A wave of laughter sounded in the room.

*   *   *

At Chittleham Farm, DC Tony Reilly parked the police car while Jane got out and walked up to the uniformed policeman standing guard outside the farmhouse. There was no sign of the black and white sheepdog today.

'Mr Peck's out in the fields, ma'am,' the policeman told Jane.

Inside the house was deathly quiet and the large farm kitchen did not look any better in daylight than it had at midnight. If anything, it was even more dirty and untidy. On the shelf above the cooker there were some photos in dusty frames of sheepdogs and prize sheep. Among them was a photo of a small group of people: Mervin looking about ten years younger. And the others were presumably his mother and father and brother?

As Jane was studying the photos, the door opened suddenly and Mervin came in.

'Can I help you?' he said in an unfriendly voice.

'Oh, hello, I was here last night,' Jane said. 'Perhaps you don't remember me?'

'What do you want?'

'I'd like to look round a bit, if you don't mind,' Jane said.

'Do I have a choice?' Mervin growled. 'Why did that woman have to lie down and die in my truck? I tell you, it's not funny. Got enough to do.'

31

'I'm afraid somebody killed her,' Jane said.

'Oh,' he said. 'Did they?'

'Can you tell me what you did during the day yesterday?' Jane asked him.

'No different from any other day. Went into Buxton for a few bits and pieces from the agricultural supplies shop in the morning. Spent the afternoon cleaning sheep's feet, feeding the animals, checking the lambs. As usual.'

'Was anyone else here?'

'No. I haven't got an alibi, if that's what you mean.' Mervin stared out of the dusty window. Jane watched his large, work-roughened hands, which were playing with a piece of yellow string and some small rubber bands. His face was reddened by the wind and rain, his hair greying and untidy. He was probably in his forties but he could have been fifty, she thought. She had not understood before that farming was such a hard life. She became aware that he was uncomfortable in her presence. But then he must have realised he was a suspect.

'Is that your brother Jack?' Jane asked, pointing to the family photo on the shelf.

'Yes,' replied Mervin.

'How often do you see him?'

'Couple of times a month, usually. He comes out at weekends to see to his bees. It's his hobby.'

'What's his job exactly?' Jane asked.

'Oh, the company makes agricultural products. But, to tell you the truth, I'm not exactly sure what it is Jack does.'

'Would you mind showing me around?' Jane asked.

Leaving Tony Reilly at the house, Jane and Mervin walked down the muddy lane to the farmyard.

'This is the sheep shed, where the lambs and ewes are,' Mervin said, leading Jane into a large, ugly, metal-roofed building on one side of a concrete yard.

Inside, the sound of the sheep bleating became suddenly deafening as they caught sight of Mervin, who usually brought their food. All Jane could see was an army of woolly coats pushing and fighting to be the first to reach what they must have hoped was a food bucket. In one corner she noticed five or six sheep separated from the rest by a large sheet of metal. They seemed to have open wounds on their faces and their heads hung low. Unlike the others, they showed no interest in the appearance of the humans.

'What's wrong with them?' Jane shouted above the noise. Even to her city eyes, these animals looked a little sick.

'Oh, just got some sort of infection,' Mervin replied. He seemed unconcerned.

Jane pointed outside to a small building on the other side of the yard. 'What's in there?' she enquired.

'A few orphan lambs,' was the blunt response.

Jane wanted to go back to the murder site, so they walked up the hill to the pick-up. From this high point there was a good view over the whole farm, and in several fields Jane could see lambs running and jumping while their mothers fed peacefully on the rich grass. Every now and again one lamb would bleat anxiously. A ewe would lift her head and answer and the lamb would go running towards her.

Looking around, Jane noticed in the distance a field containing twenty or so of the same wooden beehives she had seen the night before by the pick-up.

'Those must be your brother's bees,' she said.

'Yes,' Mervin said. 'He rents that field off me. But it's not worth it, as far as I'm concerned. Those bloody bees of his are dangerous. Go near them and they'll come after you, quick as anything.' He rubbed his arm.

Something about the place made Jane uncomfortable. Perhaps it was the idea that somewhere in this beautiful picture-postcard scene a killer was hiding. Perhaps it was something about Mervin himself. She could not decide if he was telling the truth.

On the way back to the house she said, 'There'll be a team coming out shortly to search the area for evidence.'

'Just as long as they shut the gates,' Mervin growled.

'That photo I was looking at – I'd like to borrow it please. For our records.'

'All right,' said Mervin in an unfriendly voice, 'if you must.'

Chapter 6 *An ordinary respectable woman*

Back at the police station, Jane was eating a cheese sandwich in her office when Pete walked in, holding some papers.

'Ah, you're here,' he said. 'Get anything useful?'

'I've already asked you once to knock before you come in,' Jane said shortly.

'Sorry.' There was a brief silence.

Then Jane said, 'We'll have to go and see the brother later. But . . .' She frowned.

'What? Got some ideas already?'

'No. No, it's just that farm gave me the creeps. That Mervin never looks me in the eye when he talks . . . I don't trust him.'

'He might just be shy. A lot of farmers are. They spend their days with their animals so they forget how to talk properly. They lose the power of speech,' Pete explained. He grinned suddenly. 'Especially when they're talking to an attractive young woman.'

Jane glared at him. 'You don't need to make comments like that, thank you,' she said.

'Maybe not, but it's a fact.'

She had just opened her mouth to make a suitable response when there was a knock at the office door and DS Penny Kingdom came in with the postmortem results.

'Thank you, Penny,' Jane said, glancing through the

35

report. 'Well, cause of death was a severe blow to the head with some kind of blunt instrument. Pure and simple. No suggestion of any kind of sexual attack. Nothing in the blood. Nothing else at all. An otherwise healthy individual. Time of death was sometime during the afternoon, between six and twelve hours before Mervin's 999 call. A recent insect bite, around the same sort of time, on the left hand. Probably a bee or wasp sting. Why can't they ever be more specific?'

'Must have been a bee,' Pete said. 'It's too early in the year for wasps.'

'I meant the time of death, actually,' Jane said. Was the guy being deliberately simple? 'What else? Aha! They found some bits of skin under the fingernails. We'll need a DNA test done on those. That's about it. Anyway, do you have some more information, Pete?'

'Well,' he began, 'as we know, Rose Carter lived in South Heasley.' He paused, looking through his notes.

'Yes, and . . . ?' Jane said impatiently.

'Just a minute, hold on. Ah, here we are. She taught maths and statistics part-time at the secondary school in Buxton. I'll visit the school this afternoon, and I'll also go out to South Heasley. Take some people to look round her house. See what else we can find. At the moment, it looks as if she was an ordinary, respectable sort of woman. But who knows? Maybe she had a secret life.'

'Maybe, Pete. Anything more from forensics, Penny?'

'Only that so far there's no match on the national database for the fingerprints,' Penny replied.

'So, no-one we know then. OK, off you go, and take this photo with you. As well as all this, I've got to write an operational order for a crack-down on car and house thefts. As I believe I mentioned to you before.'

Pete groaned. 'Oh that.'

'Yes. That. How about calling it "Operation Wasp"?'

'Very amusing, ma'am,' Pete said as he and Penny went out of Jane's office.

'How's it going?' Superintendent George Ferguson asked Jane a little while later as they carried their trays of tea and biscuits to a seat in the police canteen.

'OK. But it's early days yet, sir,' Jane replied. 'Shall we sit here? It seems Rose Carter was killed by a single blow to the head with something like a hammer or an iron bar. I don't think it's the work of a mentally disturbed killer – more likely someone with a more rational motive. She'd also recently been stung by a bee.'

'As far as I know, bees sting people who make them angry,' George said. 'And what makes a bee angry is being disturbed.'

'Which rather suggests that she was walking around Mervin's farm,' Jane said. 'His brother keeps bees there and, according to Mervin, they're particularly bad-tempered. But the question is, what was she doing there? Mervin insists that Rose was a complete stranger to him.'

'Is Mervin a suspect?' George asked.

'He has to be,' Jane replied. 'By his own admission, he has no alibi. He was on his own all afternoon. On the other hand, there's no obvious motive. Anyway, I'll go and see his brother later and Pete Fish should be back soon from Rose Carter's cottage. Plus, the team looking over the farm may find something. Hopefully a murder weapon, at least.'

'Well, and how is Fish, then? Behaving himself?'

'Oh well, he's a bit of a dinosaur but he's all right really. Anyway, now that he's got a real murder to deal with, he hasn't got time to annoy me.' Jane grinned. 'But they're a bit laid-back down here, aren't they?'

'You're out in the country now, don't forget,' George reminded her.

'I'm not allowed to forget it, either.' Jane laughed. 'Oops! Talk of the devil . . .' Pete Fish came into the restaurant and walked straight to their table. He seemed to be in a hurry.

'I'm sorry to interrupt, ma'am,' he said. 'I've got something you should see immediately. Do you mind?'

'Not at all. Excuse me, sir,' Jane said to George, getting up with her mouth full of biscuit.

They went to the CID office, where DC Tony Reilly and DS Penny Kingdom were sitting at a desk piled high with papers.

'I think we're really beginning to get somewhere, ma'am,' Pete began, looking pleased with himself.

'Good, let's hear it then,' Jane said.

'Well, we went to Rose's school in Buxton. She was well liked by the staff and pupils there and they're very upset. Penny spoke to a teacher called Freda Sweeney, who said she was quite close to Rose. Apparently, Rose was very keen on animals and she – that is Freda – thought that she – Rose – '

'Get on with it, Pete. Get your pronouns sorted out,' said Jane.

'My what? Oh, I see what you mean,' said Pete, slightly embarrassed. '*Rose* had joined some kind of local animal rights group.'

'Do we have a name?' Jane asked.

'No, unfortunately.'

'Also,' Penny broke in, 'Freda came out with the fact that Rose had been having an affair with a married man, only no-one's supposed to know about it. I asked her if she knew the name and she said that Rose once called him Jack.'

'Mervin's brother's name is Jack,' observed Jane.

Pete raised his eyebrows. 'You wait,' he said. 'There's more. At South Heasley, Tony and I spoke to the couple in the house next door to Rose's. Like everyone else, they are shocked by what's happened. Can't believe it. They said Rose was a wonderful woman who did a lot of work in the community. Obviously very respectable. Anyway, I asked them if they'd noticed if she'd had many visitors. Anyone regular. In small villages, you know, everyone knows what everyone else is doing.'

'Do they really? How useful,' Jane remarked. 'Where would we be without your expert knowledge of rural habits?'

Pete looked offended. 'I'm trying to be helpful here.'

'Go on.'

'Well, I said she probably had a secret life, didn't I? The neighbours said that a man used to come to visit her regularly, about once a week, sometimes more, usually in the afternoons. They didn't know who he was, but he was well-dressed, usually wore a suit. Middle-aged. Drove a white Ford Escort estate with a K registration number plate. Sometimes they'd wave to him but he always acted as if he didn't notice. We showed them the photo with Jack in and they said they thought it was the same man.'

'Time to pay a visit to Mr Jack Peck, then.' Jane said.

'Yes, ma'am. Sure is,' Pete said, doing his Texan accent. God, I hate it when he does that, Jane thought.

Penny said, 'We also got this from Rose's house.' She held up a diary.

'Well done,' Jane said. 'I'd like to look at that. Right, then, it's nearly 5.30 now. Jack Peck'll be finishing work soon, I imagine. We'd better go straight to his home.'

'Oh yes, so he will. Good idea,' Pete said.

'Thanks,' said Jane acidly.

Just then DC Maggie Pincombe joined the group. 'Thought you might like to know they've found a bike,' she announced.

'Where?' Several people said at once.

'On Mervin Peck's farm, some way from the house.'

'Any sign of a murder weapon, Maggie?' Jane asked.

'No,' said Maggie. 'Not yet.'

Chapter 7 *The beekeeper*

At about 6.45 p.m. a police car pulled up outside the suburban house in Ilford Terrace, Pilton, in the driveway of which a white K registration Ford Escort estate car was parked. Jane and Pete walked up to the front door through the tidy garden planted out with sweet-smelling roses and soft grass.

The door opened almost before they had knocked, and a tall man in his middle forties stood looking at them. He was dressed formally in a suit and tie, and his dark hair, greying at the sides, framed a face that was coldly handsome.

'Good evening, sir. CID,' Jane said, as she and Pete displayed their identity cards.

'Yes?' The man did not move.

'Are you Mr Jack Peck, brother of Mervin Peck of Chittleham Farm?'

'I am.' The voice was cautious and not very welcoming.

'We have a few questions to ask you. As you may know, a woman was found dead on your brother's farm yesterday. May we come in for a bit?' Jane asked.

'It's a little inconvenient. I have to go out soon,' Jack Peck said. 'But . . . well, all right, but I don't know what help I can give you.' He showed them into a well-furnished, comfortable room, filled with objects from foreign countries: Persian carpets, Arabic coffee pots, Chinese vases and paintings. The contrast with his brother's house was striking – the furniture was polished, the cushions smoothed, there was no dust to be seen, and a sweet smell of flowers filled the air.

'You have some lovely things here,' Jane remarked, looking around.

'Oh, collected on my travels,' Jack Peck replied.

'Does your work take you abroad, then?'

'It used to. Not any more unfortunately.'

'Do you mind me asking what you do?' Jane enquired.

'I work at Hunter Products. In the research department,' Jack told her. 'We make agricultural chemicals and animal vaccines. Not very exciting, I'm afraid.'

'Nice painting,' Pete said, pointing to a large watercolour of an attractive woman on the wall. 'Is that your wife?'

'Well, it is, as a matter of fact, but I don't know what it has to do with you. Do you have something particular to ask me?' Jack sounded impatient.

'Yes, sir.' Jane frowned at Pete. 'Do you keep bees on your brother's farm?'

'Yes. It's a hobby of mine. I can't keep them here as we don't have a big enough garden. Do I understand that you think Mervin's connected with this horrible business?'

Jane ignored his question. 'How often do you visit Chittleham Farm?' she asked.

'It depends . . . depends on the time of year and what the bees are doing. Not a lot in the winter. But they're waking up now, so about once or twice a month, I suppose, at the moment.'

'That is your car outside, I imagine, sir?' Pete said, indicating the white Ford Escort.

'It is. Look, what's all this about? I hope you don't think I had anything to do with it.'

'We have to check everything, sir,' Jane said. 'Would you mind telling me where you were yesterday afternoon?'

'I was at work. You can confirm that at the factory.'

'You didn't leave the building?'

'No, I was there all the time, I told you. You can check because all arrivals and departures of staff and visitors are recorded.'

'Did you know the dead woman, Rose Carter?' Pete enquired.

For a moment, Jack appeared about to lose control of his emotionless exterior. 'Yes,' he said quietly.

'How well?' Jane asked.

'Through my work. She does . . . I mean she did a bit of part-time statistical work for us so I used to see her from time to time to give her the material. Data analysis stuff. I'm sorry she died in such . . . unfortunate circumstances.' He spoke with difficulty.

'When did you see her last, sir?' Jane asked.

'Last Thursday, actually. I went to collect some figures from her but she hadn't quite finished the work.'

Just then, a dark green MG sports car drew up outside the house. As the driver got out, Jack said, 'That's my wife.'

Susan Peck came into the front room, carrying some large bags from local department stores. Like her husband, she was elegantly dressed, giving an impression, not of wealth exactly, but certainly of being very comfortable. Definitely a member of the town's privileged classes, Jane thought.

'Darling, these are the police. From the CID,' Jack explained.

'Oh, good evening,' Susan Peck said. 'I suppose you're here because of that poor woman on my brother-in-law's farm? I heard about it on the local news. How terrible.'

'Yes, madam,' Jane said. 'We're just going. Just for the record, where were you yesterday afternoon?'

'Excuse me . . . ?' A look of alarm appeared on Susan Peck's face.

'You were out shopping, weren't you?' Jack Peck addressed his wife. He seemed to want the interview to be concluded as rapidly as possible.

'Well . . . yes . . . I was, but . . .' Susan stammered.

'If you'll excuse us, Inspector,' Jack turned to Jane, 'we're due to meet some friends at the theatre very soon . . .'

'Of course, thank you for your help,' Jane said.

Jane and Pete walked down the garden path, while behind them the raised voices of Jack and his wife could be heard, apparently having an argument.

'She's been out spending all his hard-earned money, I reckon,' Pete said.

'Possibly,' Jane replied, unable to stop herself being annoyed by Pete's typically male remark. 'But I don't think we know all there is to know about Mr and Mrs Jack Peck yet.'

Chapter 8   *A head full of bees*

Perhaps it was a crime of passion? Jane thought to herself. Perhaps Mervin was jealous of his brother, Jack? Jane stepped out of the shower, wrapped a towel round her and went into the kitchen to make some coffee. It was a beautiful morning, the spring sunshine filled the flat.

'Breakfast, Julian?' she asked her cat, pouring him some milk while he miaowed with pleasure. 'What do you think, Julian?' she said out loud. Julian drank his milk. 'Of course, there's Susan, his wife, as well. If she knows about the affair she would have a motive. Does she have an alibi?' she asked the cat.

Jane had spent part of the previous evening looking through Rose Carter's diary. In among the shopping lists, appointments, reminders to go to the dentist, doctor and so on were some entries which needed further investigation. Jane had noticed, for example, that once a month since last November, the name of a farm appeared in the diary, such as Ladywell Farm, Upcott Farm, Beare Farm. Chittleham Farm had been the farm for February – the previous month. Did this mean that Rose had visited all these farms? On the day Rose had died the diary entry was again 'Chittleham Farm'. Why was Chittleham Farm written down twice? Was Rose, in fact, a regular visitor there?

Some of the other entries were also interesting, but

probably explained by Rose's 'working' relationship with Jack Peck. At least once a week, the initials JP and a time, such as '2.30' or '4.00', had been written. On the Thursday before Rose died, the entry read:

JP - 3.00 !!!

There was also the question of the relationship between Rose Carter and Jack Peck. It was school gossip that Rose had been having an affair, presumably with Jack Peck.

Sitting in the daily traffic jam, she planned the day. She would go to Jack's workplace herself to check out his alibi, and send Pete or one of the others out to South Heasley again. Although Rose's neighbours had seen his car regularly, or a car like his, had Jack actually been there on Monday afternoon?

After giving instructions in the CID office, Jane set off for Hunter Products. It was situated on an industrial estate on the other side of the river. As usual, the queue of traffic proceeded slowly over the bridge and Jane looked with annoyance again at the black hole by the steering wheel of her car.

Must get that fixed sometime, she thought. Since her arrival in Pilton, there didn't seem to have been a spare minute to attend to the little things that were necessary to run her life outside work. She promised herself that when this case was over, she would celebrate by going out and buying the best car stereo system she could find.

At the automatic barrier at the entrance to Hunter Products' car park, Jane spoke into a microphone, 'Detective Chief Inspector Jane Honeywell, Pilton CID.'

The word 'chief' still felt a little strange to her, but obviously not to anyone else as a faint voice replied, 'All right, madam,' and the barrier lifted. Driving in, she noticed that several closed-circuit TV cameras were positioned around the car park and high up on the factory building.

Inside the factory, the reception area was spotlessly clean and there was a hint of chemical in the air. A foxy-faced female, half hidden behind a high reception counter, asked Jane, 'Can I help you?'

Jane showed her ID and asked to speak to the person in charge. 'This is a murder enquiry,' she added quickly in case the woman had any idea of putting her off.

'I'll see what I can do,' the receptionist said, and picked up a phone. She talked quietly into it for a minute or two and then told Jane, 'Mrs Keane will be down in a minute. Please have a seat.' She gestured in the direction of a large red leather sofa.

After about five minutes, a tall woman dressed in a white silk suit came through the only door leading from the reception area.

'Jo Keane, Managing Director. What can I do for you?' She smiled. Her clear blue eyes were set a little close together in an otherwise attractive face framed by soft dark curls. Jane thought they must be around the same age.

She shook the extended hand. 'DCI Jane Honeywell,' she said. 'I'm looking into the murder incident out at Chittleham Farm, which you may have heard about. I believe Chittleham Farm belongs to the brother of one of your employees. I wonder if you could spare me a minute or two?'

Jo Keane looked briefly at her Rolex watch. 'I've got a couple of minutes, but that's all, I'm afraid. How can I help?'

'Thank you,' said Jane. 'Can you confirm that Mr Jack Peck works here?'

'He does,' replied Jo Keane. 'He's one of our key people. He's a research scientist in the animal vaccine department.'

'Has he worked here long?'

'Oh, I'm not sure exactly without checking. A few years. Before he came to us he was with a chemical company, based in Africa. I believe they were working on a vaccine for malaria.'

'Was Mr Peck at work last Monday?' Jane asked.

'As far as I know. If he went out, it'll be in the record. I'll have it brought down for you.' Jo Keane turned to the receptionist and asked her to fetch a copy of Monday's records.

'Would it be possible for someone to leave the building without anyone knowing, say, for an hour or two?' Jane asked while they waited for the receptionist to return.

'No, I don't think so. We're a small company here. We all more or less know what each other is doing.'

The receptionist reappeared and handed Jane several sheets of computer paper. 'You keep very careful records,' remarked Jane, looking through the papers. There was no indication that she could see of Jack's having left the factory after his arrival at work at 8.45 a.m. on Monday.

'Well, we like to know who comes in and out,' explained Mrs Keane.

'Would you mind if I borrowed the videos from the closed circuit system?' Jane asked.

'Well . . .' Jo Keane hesitated.

'I'm just interested in the car park and the entrances and

exits to the building,' Jane said. 'I'll only need them for 24 hours or so.'

'Well, OK. I'll have them sent round to the police station,' Jo Keane said finally, with a stiff smile.

*   *   *

Later, as Jane sat at her desk staring at the computer print-outs from Hunter Products on one side of her desk and a half-written operational order for Operation Wasp on the other, there was a knock at the door and Pete came in.

'You knocked, which is an improvement, but you're also supposed to wait until I say come in, you know,' Jane remarked.

'Sorry,' said Pete, not really listening. 'I've just got back from South Heasley. That family photo, I showed it to another of Rose's neighbours, Mary Brady, who wasn't at home the first time we went. Not only did she recognise Jack but she also saw a white Escort estate outside Rose's house early Monday afternoon. She didn't see the driver but she was positive it was Jack's car. So, he's been lying to us. That means he has something to hide. I think we've got a prime suspect here.'

'Erm . . . unfortunately for us, he has a perfect alibi,' Jane said. 'He was at work all afternoon. It's all in there.' She indicated the papers on her desk. Pete's grin changed to a look of some disappointment. 'Anyway, why would he want to kill Rose?'

'Easy,' said Pete. 'They had an argument, maybe she said he should leave his wife, he lost his temper, he hit her on the head with . . . I don't know, a hammer, then he got rid of her body on his brother's farm.'

'Why there?'

'I don't know, people do odd things. Perhaps he had to go there anyway to check his bees?' Pete sounded unconvinced himself.

'But I told you, he didn't leave the factory all afternoon,' Jane said.

'Are we sure?' Pete asked.

'More or less but I'm going to check the closed circuit TV videos at home tonight. Just to be absolutely certain.'

'Want any help?' Pete offered. Jane looked at him, noticing that his resistance towards her had softened. She wondered why.

'I don't think so, thanks.' She valued her privacy. In any case there was a large pile of washing-up in the sink, and the bathroom needed cleaning, and last night's dinner things were still on the sitting room table. 'But if you need something to do, you could see if you can get some names of animal rights groups operating in the area.'

'Yes, ma'am,' Pete said with an ironic smile.

Back at her flat, Jane went straight to the fridge. As she had thought, there was nothing to eat for dinner. She tried the freezer. A frozen lasagne. That would do. She put it in the microwave, poured herself a large glass of red Rioja wine and settled down in front of the TV to watch several hours of video film of the car parks and exits and entrances at Hunter Products Ltd.

The film ran silently on and on for what felt like a lifetime. Jane found herself thinking that Hunter Products seemed to be very security conscious. What were they worried about? Industrial spies? She was beginning to feel sleepy when suddenly she thought she could see a figure who looked like Jack Peck walking across the car park. The person was getting into a P registration MG sports car. She played the film again, to be sure. There was no doubt about it. It was definitely him. The time on the video said 17.10. Of course! Why hadn't she thought of that before? The Pecks had two cars. So, if Jack Peck had used his wife's car last Monday to go to work, his wife could have taken his car, the Escort estate. And the car had been seen outside Rose's cottage on Monday afternoon . . .

That night Jane slept badly. Once she woke, sweating, and realised she had been dreaming. She had been running and running, through fields and streams, climbing over gates and hedges. On a road a motorist stopped and she got into the car. It was Pete. 'Are you all right?' he asked. 'No,' she answered, 'I have to get away from the swans.' She looked out of the back window and saw, following the car, a small black cloud which seemed to be getting larger and larger as it caught up with them. The cloud turned out to be a swarm of bees. She woke up when bees started appearing inside the car.

Chapter 9 *The good news and the bad news*

At 8.30 the next morning, Jane was sitting in Superintendent George Ferguson's office. Of the two things she needed to discuss with him, reporting on the Rose Carter case would be, she thought, a fairly easy task.

'I think we have three possible suspects,' Jane told George. 'There's the farmer Mervin Peck, who lives on Chittleham Farm and had plenty of opportunity, but no obvious motive. Then there's Jack Peck, his brother, and his wife Susan. They both have alibis, but I have the feeling one of them is hiding something.'

'What about forensic evidence?' George asked.

'Well, that would provide the key, I think, if we could get some DNA samples, some hair or skin. If none of the suspects will give samples willingly, we'll either have to make some arrests or do something a bit clever.'

'I'll leave it in your hands, Jane.' George smiled at her.

The second matter was a little more tricky: in order to have sufficient staff and money for Operation Wasp, Jane needed to get George's agreement to a reduction in the zero tolerance activities.

'The thing is, sir,' Jane explained, 'a lot of car crime and burglaries are committed by people from out of town. I'd like to try an experiment for a month or two with some road blocks and observation teams – just to see what happens, see if we can reduce the car crime and burglaries.'

'Well, OK then. Give it a try for two months,' George said reluctantly. 'But remember, the public like zero tolerance – it gets the drunks off the streets for one thing.'

After her meeting with George, Jane set off for 23 Ilford Terrace. The green MG sports car was outside the house.

Susan Peck came to the front door and frowned slightly when she saw who her visitor was.

'I'm sorry to disturb you, madam, but I need to speak to you for a moment,' Jane said. 'Can I come in, please?'

Susan Peck turned wordlessly and walked back into her kitchen. She switched off the radio and looked at Jane expectantly.

'On Tuesday, you told us you were out shopping the previous afternoon,' Jane began.

'That's right.'

'Where did you go?'

'To the supermarket, and maybe one or two other places.'

'Where exactly?' Jane insisted.

'I don't remember. I had one or two calls to make. Why?'

'Did you use your husband's car to do these things?' Jane asked her.

'Yes. I always use it when I go to the supermarket. You can't get much in the MG.'

Jane took a breath. 'Mrs Peck, why did you visit Rose Carter last Monday? There's no point denying it,' she added as Susan Peck seemed about to protest. 'You were seen by the neighbours.' This was not completely true but it was worth trying. It worked.

Susan Peck sat down suddenly, her head in her hands

and her shoulders shaking. She appeared to be weeping soundlessly.

'OK.' She looked up, tears welling up in her eyes. 'I suppose I have to tell you. I went to see Rose Carter because I was sure that my husband was having an affair with her. They've known each other for years, and shortly after she moved down here a couple of years ago, Jack became very . . . I don't know, distant towards me. He seemed to be spending a lot of time at her house, working or so he said. But her perfume was on his clothes . . .' At this point, the tears started to run freely down her reddened cheeks.

'I'm sorry,' Susan Peck said after a little, managing to recover her self-control. 'Look, I didn't kill Rose. We just talked for a bit. She told me that she had lately made a decision to stop the relationship. Then she rode off on her bike saying she had something to do. She used to cycle everywhere, I believe.'

'What time was this?' Jane enquired.

'About 3 p.m., I think.'

'Did Rose give a reason for breaking off the relationship with your husband?' Jane asked.

'No,' Susan Peck said. 'She wouldn't say.' After a pause, she said nervously, 'Does this make me a suspect?'

'Well, Mrs Peck, so far it looks as if you were the last person to see Rose alive,' Jane pointed out. 'However, if you agree to provide a DNA sample, we could take you off the list.'

'Oh . . .' Susan Peck looked alarmed.

'We just take a sample of your saliva. It's not painful. I'll send someone round, then?'

Susan Peck nodded. 'All right,' she murmured.

*   *   *

Jane Honeywell's team of detectives was all present when she walked into the CID office a little while later.

'Well, would you like the good news?' she asked them. 'Mrs Peck has agreed to give us a DNA sample.'

'What's the bad news then?' Tony Reilly asked.

'The bad news is that we still have nothing that's really any use,' Jane said. 'Nothing that adds up to anything. Jack Peck's alibi seems to stand up, and I don't really think Susan Peck's a likely suspect.' Jane sat down heavily at one of the desks. 'OK, who's going to go and get a DNA sample from Mervin Peck . . . ?'

They were saved from having to volunteer by the telephone.

'Detective Chief Inspector Honeywell,' Jane said into the phone. 'What can I do for you?'

'Oh,' a female voice said. There was a short pause. 'Um . . . my name is Elisa Scott. I knew Rose Carter. I don't know whether it's important, but I think I may know why she was out on that farm where they found her.'

'Yes?' Jane said. 'Please go on.'

'Well, Rose belonged to our organisation, PAW, Project for Animal Welfare,' Elisa Scott explained. Her voice was quiet and gentle and without the local accent.

'And what's that exactly?' Jane asked.

'Well,' came the reply, 'mainly, we go around looking for cases of animals being badly treated and reporting them. We do a lot of the legwork for the RSPCA and . . . er . . . it's a little complicated . . .' The pleasant voice hesitated.

'Just tell me about Rose, then,' Jane said.

'OK,' Elisa continued. 'Each member in the branch is responsible for a particular area. What you do is you go round the farms in your area checking up that the farmer is looking after his animals properly. Chittleham Farm was in Rose's area and she went there about a month ago. She reported after her visit that she was worried about some of the sheep there and that perhaps she should go back again sometime. Then I saw her last Friday and she said she was going to go out to Chittleham Farm for another look. Maybe the farmer found her and . . .' Again the voice paused.

'Ms Scott,' said Jane, 'I have to go out to Chittleham Farm in about half an hour anyway. Would you like to come with me? You could show me exactly why your group is so concerned about the animals on Mervin Peck's farm.'

'Of course, whatever you want,' Elisa Scott replied.

Jane put the phone down and turned to her team. 'OK,' she said. 'I'll have a go at persuading Mervin Peck to supply a DNA sample while I'm at the farm. And Pete, can you organise the DNA test for Mrs Peck, please?'

Chapter 10   *The suspect's got a gun*

'How long had Rose been a member of your group?' Jane asked Elisa as they drove towards Chittleham Farm.

'Well, not long actually. Since about last October, I think. I met her at a party and we got talking. Then one day she just walked in and said she wanted to be involved.'

'Tell me more about PAW,' Jane said.

'Well . . .' Elisa began, a little hesitantly.

'Are you one of these groups which employ what I would call "doubtful methods"?'

'You mean illegal? Sometimes, I suppose we're a little aggressive,' Elisa said. 'You wouldn't believe some of the things that go on. There are puppy farms where they keep little dogs in cages in buildings far away from anywhere with no food or drink or daylight. We don't warn anyone we're coming so we can catch them doing things to animals which they shouldn't.'

Jane looked quickly from the road to Elisa with some surprise. The soft voice had suddenly filled with the passion felt by someone for whom the end completely justified the means.

'You mean that you break in?' Jane asked.

'Er . . . well, I shouldn't say so to you, I suppose, but yes, we do if we think we have to.'

'I didn't hear that!' Jane told her. 'So is it possible that the farmer at Chittleham Farm had never seen Rose Carter before the afternoon she was killed?'

'Yes, it's quite likely. We prefer to go in and out without being seen.'

Jane wondered how Elisa had learnt her skills in this kind of work.

'I was in the army,' Elisa said, answering Jane's thoughts. 'Briefly.'

At Chittleham Farm, there was no sign of the sheepdog. Jane decided Mervin must be out in the fields somewhere.

'All right,' she said to Elisa. 'Let's see if we can find out what was bothering Rose about the sheep.'

'Well, we won't miss it if there's anything wrong,' Elisa said. 'The sheep'll look terrible. Thin. Wool hanging off. They may have wounds on them, or they may be lying down and not get up when you go near them.'

They passed the small wooden building in which Mervin had said there were orphan lambs. 'Let's have a quick look in here while we're passing,' Jane said, opening the door. 'Um . . . I think this might be what Rose was after,' she declared.

Elisa looked over Jane's shoulder and drew her breath in sharply. 'Oh my goodness,' she said pushing past Jane. The five or six sheep inside did not move or raise their heads as she approached them. They were lying on the floor, still breathing but almost lifeless. The air was thick with an evil mix of smells: chemicals and diseased flesh.

'These are seriously sick animals. I don't know what's wrong with them but they shouldn't be here. They could have a disease which should be reported to the authorities . . .' Elisa's voice died away as she suddenly glanced at a point behind Jane.

Jane turned and found herself looking into the barrel of

a shotgun. It was aimed directly at her and Mervin Peck was the one aiming it. He did not look as if he was just out for an afternoon's game shooting.

'You have no right to be in here. Get out. I know my rights, you should have a search warrant to come in here, nosing around,' he growled.

'I'm afraid you're wrong there, Mr Peck,' Jane said calmly. 'This is a crime scene, and you are obstructing a police officer.' She felt in her bag, found her mobile phone and started to call. Mervin turned and ran outside, towards an old car parked in the yard. Jane followed but stopped when Mervin pointed the gun at her again.

'Don't move or I'll shoot,' he shouted. She had no option but to watch as he climbed into the ancient vehicle. Surprisingly, the engine burst into life and he drove quickly away up the lane.

Elisa, who had been examining the sick animals more closely, reappeared in the yard. 'Come on,' Jane shouted. 'I'm going after him.' They ran to Jane's car and jumped in. At the top of the lane they saw Mervin turn left down a road that led towards Buxton.

'I know a short cut,' Elisa said. 'Go down this lane. We can cut him off.'

'We need some help,' Jane said, holding the steering wheel with one hand while trying to operate her mobile phone with the other. The car was moving rapidly towards a ditch.

'Watch out,' Elisa cried. 'Give me that thing. I'll do it. You watch the road.'

While Elisa held the mobile phone, Jane screamed into it above the noise of the car engine: 'I need assistance urgently. Don't ask me to explain, just get some armed cars out here fast. The suspect's got a gun.' She told them where they were and switched off the phone.

The lane was just wide enough for one car. On each side was a high bank with a thick hedge on top and, at its base, a ditch. The lane twisted and turned, up and down hills and it was impossible to know whether or not there was a vehicle coming in the other direction. Jane could not see further than a few metres ahead and was able to drive at only 30 kph. At every bend in the road she just hoped for the best.

Without warning, the lane suddenly opened out onto a crossroads. Before Jane realised what was happening, Mervin's car shot across the road just in front of them. To avoid hitting Mervin's vehicle, she had to brake sharply. The wheels of the Mazda hit the stony edge of the lane and the car turned through ninety degrees, slid sideways and came to a complete stop with one front wheel in the ditch. The bottom of the engine was resting on the road surface while the other front wheel spun uselessly in the air.

'Are you all right?' Jane asked Elisa. Elisa nodded. Jane then turned off the engine and cursed, 'Bloody hell!' She got out to examine the car. As she stared in frustration at the river of oil flowing out from underneath the car, the sound of police sirens suddenly filled the air. They seemed to be approaching from all directions, including Buxton, where Mervin was now headed. Jane realised that there was a strong likelihood that at least one car would meet Mervin head on, coming the other way.

Just then a police car appeared on the road that Mervin had come along, its blue light flashing and the siren sounding. Jane waved it down and jumped in as it slowed.

'Quick,' she shouted. 'He's gone down there.'

A little further down the road they turned a corner and came across Mervin's car. It was positioned at an angle across the narrow lane, its nose buried in the high bank.

'Well, well,' Jane remarked to her driver. 'Looks like they've got him.'

Black marks on the surface of the road showed where the car had slid to a stop. By the side of a parked police car, a uniformed police gunman was holding a gun aimed at Mervin's car. As Jane watched, Mervin got out, his shaking hands held high.

Chapter 11 *The confession*

Detective Chief Inspector Jane Honeywell walked into the interview room and felt suddenly certain that the man sitting at the table was the one responsible for the death of Rose Carter. There was something about the look of the muscular shoulders, the way the large rough hands played on the table, and the deadness in the unfocussed eyes which stared blankly towards the floor.

Pete followed her in and stood behind her as she took a chair and faced Mervin Peck, who was accompanied by a lawyer.

'This interview is being tape recorded . . .' Jane repeated the required words as she had done so many times before. 'I am interviewing . . . would you please say your full name?' She looked at Mervin and waited.

Eventually Mervin muttered at the floor, 'Mervin Donald Peck.'

Then Jane stated the time and date and finished by saying, 'This interview may be given in evidence if your case is brought to trial. You do not have to say anything. But it may harm your defence if you do not mention when questioned something which you later rely on in court. Anything which you do say may be given in evidence.'

As she spoke, Jane was watching Mervin closely. He looked pale, and sweat appeared on his nose and forehead.

She began her questions. 'Mr Peck, when you were

arrested earlier, you refused to explain why you threatened me with a gun. Would you care to tell me now?' Mervin did not respond.

Jane tried again. 'Mr Peck, I think you may have some information concerning the death of Rose Carter.' Again there was no answer. Instead Mervin suddenly gripped his arm as if in pain.

'Mr Peck, you're in serious trouble. You will be charged with threatening a police officer. We will then be in a position to collect a DNA sample from you, which we can compare with samples we have taken from the scene of the crime. If there is a positive match, then you will also be charged with her murder. It would save everyone a lot of time and trouble if you would tell us what we need to know now.'

Mervin looked at his solicitor, who nodded.

'All right, I'll tell you what you want.' Mervin's voice sounded rough, like boots walking over moorland stones. 'I have this temper. Sometimes it gets the better of me . . . It was about 4.30 in the afternoon. I was in the shed doing the sheep as usual, you know, feeding and watering and that. Came outside and thought I heard someone shout. Went round the side of the building and she was there looking at her hand and rubbing it. She must've been stung by a bee or something, I don't know. She said she was going to report me for not looking after my sheep properly. Told her to get off my land. She just laughed at me. I went towards her and she picked up an old axe that was lying around. She must've thought I was going to do something to her. I tried to pull the axe away from her. She was screaming at me and I went wild. My arm was bad, see.

63

The next thing I knew I'd got the axe from her and hit her with the side of it. She fell immediately and was quiet. Hadn't meant to hit her. Just seemed to lose control somehow. It was an accident, really it was. Didn't mean to do it . . .' The words died away.

'Go on, Mr Peck,' Jane told him.

'Don't remember too clearly,' Mervin continued. 'I knew the boy was coming soon so I'd have to hide her. Thought of the pick-up truck, which I'd left in the top field earlier. Carried her up there and covered her with a tarpaulin. And I put an old beehive on the top that was lying about in the field. To stop the tarpaulin blowing off, see? Was going to take her up to where there's an old tin mine on the moor later, after dark.'

Sweat was by this time pouring down Mervin's ash-coloured face. He asked for some water and drank it rapidly. Jane became aware of a strange, unpleasant smell coming from him.

'And what did you do after that?' she asked him.

'The boy arrived and we had a lot to do, with the ewes lambing and all. Later I went back in the house for something to eat and a bit of a sit-down, but I must have fallen asleep. The next thing I know is the boy is pulling at my arm saying I had to go outside with him.'

'Mr Peck, would you please speak up? Now, are you certain you had never seen Rose Carter before?' Jane asked.

'No,' Mervin said. 'But I know who she is now.' He laughed in a cracked, broken fashion. 'She's my brother's fancy woman, that's what. He phoned me the day after they took her away and it was on the local news. He was upset because it was his girlfriend that had been found on my farm. Told him he should be grateful.'

'What do you mean, Mr Peck? Grateful?'

Mervin looked confused for a moment. 'I mean . . . I mean, my brother's got a wife. It's not right to carry on with other women, is it?' he stammered.

'I guess you're right, Mr Peck,' Jane said. 'Tell me, if it was an accident, why didn't you call the police?'

'Don't know. I panicked, couldn't think straight. My arm was giving me trouble, see, and I'd been up all the night before with the sheep. S'pose I thought that no-one had seen me, no-one would know. Seemed easier to get rid of the body, less trouble . . .'

'Where is the axe now?'

'At the bottom of the hole where I throw dead lambs and that kind of thing.' Mervin fell silent. He gripped his arm and gave a groan of pain. Jane realised suddenly that the man was probably quite ill. His eyes were over bright and he was plainly feverish. He stared up at her and she saw in his eyes the same expression as she had seen in his sick sheep. She didn't know if it was the look of a troubled conscience or of fever. Or both.

'Mr Peck, are you feeling all right?'

'No, as it happens. Can't stand this pain in my arm much longer,' he whispered.

Mervin's lawyer glanced at Jane and opened his mouth but she spoke first. 'All right then, we'd better stop for a bit so a doctor can take a look at you,' she said.

'Well, that was all rather strange,' Jane remarked to Pete a little while later, after the police doctor had examined Mr Peck. The doctor confirmed that he was indeed not well enough to be questioned and arranged for him to be admitted to the local hospital.

'What do you mean?' Pete asked.

'Well, he's obviously quite ill for one thing. But that's not what I mean, really,' Jane said. 'From what he says he has an uncontrollable temper and he'll use violence, and he's quite prepared to throw a dead person into a hole like one of his sheep. Yet he disapproves of his brother having an affair. The man has a rather twisted sense of right and wrong.'

'Listen,' Pete said. 'Farmers work with animals. They're used to violence. Nature is violent. Up on the moor on his own all the time. Only talking from time to time with a boy who's simple, not seeing another human being for days, it's not surprising that things get out of proportion.'

'I suppose you're right,' Jane said slowly. 'But I still think there's something not quite right about all this. It seems odd that he hit her on the head simply because he lost his temper.'

'We don't need to worry about that,' Pete said. 'We've got the confession on tape. He's told us where to find the murder weapon. As soon as he's recovered we can charge him and it'll go to court with no problem. That's it. Come on, let's go and celebrate in the pub. I'll buy you whatever you want.'

'Well, that's some offer.' Jane laughed.

'I mean, whatever you want to *drink*,' Pete said, going a little red.

'We haven't charged him yet. Isn't it a little too early to start celebrating?' she remarked.

'Never mind about that. Come on, let's go and relax now. We deserve it.'

'I've got to get my car fixed,' Jane said.

'You don't need to worry about that, either. It's already in the garage for our mechanics to look at,' Pete smiled. Jane looked at him in some surprise. How thoughtful of him to have arranged that for her.

*   *   *

It was well after 6 o'clock when Jane ordered a red wine in the pub and found a table. Pete followed behind her with a large glass of beer.

'Er . . .' Pete began as they sat down. 'This case, ma'am. It's kind of hard for me to say this but I'm impressed with the way you've handled it. You know, I was hoping for your job myself, so I wasn't too pleased when they gave it to someone else, especially . . .'

'Especially what?' Jane said, knowing what he would say. She could read him like a book.

'Well, you know we're a bit old-fashioned around here . . .'

'And?'

'And well, I guess I shouldn't say this kind of thing these days, but I really didn't think it was a woman's job. But, um, I can see I was wrong. Prejudiced . . .' There was a pause in the conversation.

'Where's a good place to get a car stereo?' Jane said suddenly.

He smiled at her, showing a row of even white teeth. 'Well, as it happens I know someone with a shop. If you need advice on stereos, you can rely on me . . .' He was clearly relieved to be talking about a familiar subject.

Jane looked at him closely for the first time since they had had their difference of opinion last Monday morning.

He was quite attractive, really. He had a nice smile and a pleasant face, though he somehow reminded her of a reptile. Perhaps it was the slightly heavy eyelids. Also he could do with losing a bit of weight.

'You must be joking,' she exclaimed. 'Rely on you? I'd as soon rely on a man-eating crocodile.'

'Don't you mean person-eating?'

'Oh, ha ha, very amusing.' Jane pulled a face at him. 'Anyway, now this is over, you lot are going to be starting on Operation Wasp: road checkpoints, watching car parks, the lot . . . I'll tell you about it tomorrow.' Jane gave a half smile.

Just then her mobile phone rang. It was Maggie Pincombe. 'The hospital's just phoned,' she said. 'Apparently, Mervin Peck's quite poorly. His condition has worsened.'

'I'll go and see him before I go home,' said Jane. 'I've got a bad feeling about this.'

'I'll come with you,' Pete offered.

'Don't worry,' Jane said. 'You go on home and relax.'

'OK, but I'll drive you to the hospital first. Don't forget, you're without a car.' Again Pete flashed his charming smile.

'All right, then. Thanks,' Jane replied.

Chapter 12 *A nasty open wound*

'Oh, come on,' Jane said to Pete after they had they pulled up outside the main entrance to Pilton Hospital, a large, grey, unattractive building on the northern edge of the town. 'You might as well come in now you're here.'

They waited at the reception desk inside while the receptionist tried to find Mervin, both agreeing that they hated hospitals, and especially their smell. Apparently, Mervin was in an observation ward. They took the lift to the top floor and went through swing doors into a ward used for patients whose illnesses were still being investigated. Tonight there were only a few occupants and Pete and Jane passed several empty bays of half a dozen beds each as they walked down the silent corridor. Some way beyond the nurses' desk, a young uniformed policewoman was reading a newspaper in a space just off the corridor.

'Mr Peck?' Jane asked.

'In there.' The WPC pointed to a door. Jane opened the door to the single room and looked in. Mervin Peck seemed to be asleep. A long tube was attached to his good arm and the other was resting on the bedclothes, heavily bandaged. Jane closed the door again quietly.

From the other end of the corridor a young man in a white coat appeared, the sound of his shoes on the polished floors exaggerated by the silence. 'Hello, I'm Dr Fahid. Can I help you?'

'What's the matter with him?' Pete enquired, nodding his head towards Mervin Peck's door.

'We're not sure yet,' replied the doctor. 'He has a nasty open wound on his arm. He told us a bee stung him originally and the wound never healed. It simply got worse and worse. We're a bit concerned that he might have blood poisoning. He's running a high fever.'

'No wonder he looked a bit sick earlier,' Jane remarked.

'Yes, it's a long time since I've seen a wound quite like this,' Dr Fahid went on. 'The last time was when I was in West Africa just after I qualified as a doctor and I got caught up in the middle of a war. My own opinion is that he might have gas gangrene.'

'What's that?' asked Jane.

'Well, gangrene basically means that part of the body dies,' Dr Fahid explained. 'First there is pain and then the part of the body turns black and there's often a bad smell. In the case of gas gangrene, it's caused by a particular type of bacteria. Quite nasty.'

'Oh,' Jane said, surprised. 'So what's the cure?'

'Well, usually you have to treat the affected part by cutting it off, which means he might lose his arm. I'm afraid Mr Peck was rather upset when we told him about that. Anyway,' Dr Fahid went on, 'we've done some blood tests. We'll have the results in a day or two. Meanwhile, hopefully we can keep him stable.'

On their way out of the hospital, Jane and Pete were met by a familiar figure.

'Good evening, Inspector,' Jack Peck smiled stiffly, 'I hear you're holding my brother. Where is he, please? I'd like to see him.'

'*Chief* Inspector, actually,' Jane responded. 'I'm afraid that's not possible, Mr Peck. We still need to question him. And at present he's too ill to see anyone anyway.'

Jack Peck looked thoughtful. After a moment, he said, 'Well, as his brother, surely I have a right to enquire about his health? Who should I talk to?'

'He's in the care of Dr Fahid. Ask at reception. They should be able to find him for you,' Jane told him.

*   *   *

Jane spent Friday dealing with routine matters at the station, and completing her plans and briefing the CID department for Operation Wasp. The other departments involved would be informed of the plans on Monday so that the operation could begin the following week. As far as Mervin was concerned, they could do nothing more until he recovered and could be charged, so she put the case to the back of her mind and went home for the weekend.

On Saturday the weather was grey and wet – a good day to do some decorating. She put on her oldest jeans in order to do some serious cleaning and painting. Together with cooking, this was one of the few ways in which she was able to relax. Later, she would go to the supermarket and buy the ingredients for one of her favourite meals, Thai spinach soup followed by a hot prawn curry.

She stood by her sitting room window, looking out across the river. The gently flowing water reflected the iron grey of the clouds above it, and its smooth surface was broken by small splashes of rain. The swans had long gone, probably guarding their nests somewhere, Jane thought. Instead, seagulls floated and dived, their sad cries echoing in the damp air as they fought over pieces of rubbish on the water.

The evening was one of those times that Jane treasured. She was happy with her own company and, alone, was able to arrange her time as she wanted. She put some music on, prepared her food and settled down on the sofa with Julian the cat for a Saturday evening's TV entertainment. She didn't often watch TV. Tonight, however, she felt like simply sitting and looking at whatever was on, whatever would take her into a different world from the one in which she spent most of her waking hours.

As it happened, the first programme she saw was a game show in which young men and women had to answer questions and were rewarded with the holiday of their dreams. After that, there was a popular detective series. This she could not bear – it was too much like work, and anyway the TV writers never got everyday life in a police station exactly right. So she changed channels and found herself looking at a serious documentary programme about sudden outbreaks of previously unknown diseases. The screen showed pictures of an unnamed country somewhere in the developing world. There were scenes typical of remote places in Africa: women making flour and small, fascinated children staring up at the cameras. 'In 1976,' the voice told her, 'Ebola Fever suddenly appeared in the Sudan and in Zaire. This disease is a killer, having a death rate of around eighty per cent. The victim suffers from headaches, fever and internal bleeding and usually dies after about eight days.'

The picture changed to a close-up of a mosquito injecting its long needle-like tongue into human skin. 'Rift

Valley Fever,' the voice cheerfully continued, 'is another unpleasant disease, which causes bleeding and brain fever. It is carried by mosquitoes. At one time it was found in areas around the Sahara desert and was mainly limited to domestic animals such as cattle, sheep and goats. But, in 1977, 600 people died of this disease in Egypt. It seems likely that there is now a new variety of the original disease which affects humans and which threatens to spread to other areas in the Middle East, and even beyond.'

The voice went on and Jane found herself becoming sleepy. She reached for the TV remote control. 'Bed-time,' she told Julian. She looked again at the screen briefly. Now the film showed scientists in white coats examining tubes of liquid.

'We don't know how or why these diseases suddenly appear with such fatal consequences,' one of the scientists was explaining. 'But at present there are no-one hundred per cent effective cures.'

Then came loud music and pictures of war planes.

'For this reason,' the scientist went on, 'these illnesses are ideally suited for biological warfare . . .'

Jane pressed the remote control. She had enough to think about without worrying about the possible destruction of the world by biological warfare. She would leave that to someone else to deal with.

Chapter 13 *Another call in the night*

At around three o'clock on Sunday morning the telephone rang next to Jane's bed. At first she thought it was her alarm clock going off and she threw out an arm in order to switch it off. Then she realised that it was the phone and picked up the receiver.

'Yes?' she mumbled, half asleep.

'Sorry to wake you, ma'am, it's Pete here.'

'And?'

'We've just had a call from the hospital. Mervin Peck is dead.'

'What? Oh my God.' Jane was wide awake now. 'OK, I'll be there as soon as I can.'

'There's no need . . .'

'No, I'll come immediately. I'll see you in around half an hour. Send a car for me, will you?'

When Jane arrived at the hospital, she found Pete talking to the young woman police constable who had been on guard outside Mervin's room. The WPC seemed close to tears.

'I'm sorry, I'm so sorry,' she kept on repeating.

'This is WPC Morgan,' Pete explained. 'She's just recently joined the police. Only just finished college.' He rolled his eyes towards the ceiling. 'Tell the DCI what happened,' Pete asked the constable.

'Well, ma'am,' WPC Morgan began. 'Everything was

fine. It was just a little after midnight. The nurse had just been in to see Mr Peck and I was reading a book outside his room. And then this doctor came along and told me there was a phone call for me at the desk. I stood up and started to walk towards the nurses' desk and the next thing I know is someone has grabbed me from behind and put something which smelled like a chemical over my face. I passed out and didn't wake up till a nurse shook me awake a little while ago.'

'What did the doctor look like?' Pete asked.

'Um . . . shoulder-length blonde hair and glasses. About thirty, I'd say. Quite tall, but I was sitting down . . .'

'How do you know she was a doctor?' Jane asked her.

'Well, she looked like one. She was wearing a white coat and all.' WPC Morgan looked miserable.

'Had you seen her before?'

'No, ma'am, I don't think so.'

At this point Dr Fahid and a couple of nurses appeared. 'This is terrible,' Dr Fahid said. He was plainly very upset.

'Just tell me anything you can think of, even if you can't think of a reason why it might be important,' Jane told him.

'Well, I saw Mr Peck at about three o'clock yesterday afternoon. He was stable and quite comfortable and he seemed to have calmed down a lot. That's all . . .' Dr Fahid turned to the nurses at his side.

One of the nurses spoke. 'Someone came to the desk to ask about him at about five o'clock. A man. Tall, smart-looking. I thought they might be related or something.'

'Probably his brother,' Dr Fahid interrupted. 'I spoke to him downstairs on Thursday night.'

'Anyway,' the nurse went on, 'I told him Mr Peck was a little better and then he went.'

'Any other visitors?' Jane asked.

'Only his lawyer on Friday,' the nurse said.

'So who was the last to see Mr Peck alive?' Jane enquired.

The other nurse spoke. 'I gave him his medicine at around ten o'clock when I came on duty. He seemed OK then. He was quiet, anyway. I looked in at about midnight and he was asleep.'

'And was it you who discovered that Mervin was dead?'

She nodded unhappily. 'Yes, I came along to take his temperature and blood pressure at around half past two and I noticed that the WPC here seemed to be asleep so I tried to wake her up. She was sitting on the chair but she looked like she was about to fall off. She wouldn't wake up at first so I started to think that something might be wrong. After a bit she came round but she was very shaky and confused, and she started mumbling something about a doctor and a phone call. I left her there while I went in to check Mr Peck but . . . he was dead. I got Dr Fahid up here immediately and we called the police.'

'Have you had a look at him, Dr Fahid?' Jane asked.

'Yes,' Dr Fahid replied. 'I did a quick examination. I noticed that he was blue around the mouth, which can often mean that someone has been suffocated, but there were no signs of a struggle, which is a little odd.'

'OK,' Jane said, turning to Pete. 'I want the post-mortem done as soon as possible. Tell them to phone the results through to us as a matter of urgency. And get on to personnel here and find out who this blonde female doctor is.'

Chapter 14 *An undesirable situation*

'This is all rather unfortunate, Jane,' George Ferguson was saying, looking serious as she stood in his office on Monday morning.

Though mildly expressed, George's disapproval stung and Jane tried to offer a defence. 'I agree, sir, it's an extremely undesirable situation and I'm desperately sorry that it's happened. The trouble is, the security's not very good at the hospital. It turns out that there is a service lift right next to Mr Peck's room, for example. Also I'm afraid the WPC on duty was rather inexperienced. But we'll do our best to sort it out, sir.'

'I'm sure you will, Jane,' George responded.

Jane went down to CID where she found her staff looking depressed.

'What the hell's going on, ma'am?' DC Tony Reilly asked. 'Is someone trying to make us look like idiots?'

'Looks like it,' Jane replied bluntly, drawing a plan of the top floor of the hospital on the whiteboard.

'OK. Now listen up, everyone,' she began. 'Whoever murdered Mervin Peck in his hospital bed knew exactly what they were doing. This was a very carefully planned operation. WPC Morgan was attacked from behind, here, just by the passage leading to Mr Peck's room, as she started to walk down the corridor towards the nurses' desk. Notice that there is a service lift which opens immediately onto the corridor just beyond the side room where Mr Peck was. It's likely that the attacker escaped that way.'

'Excuse me, ma'am,' DC Maggie Pincombe spoke up, 'but did the blonde doctor come from that direction also, from the lift?'

'WPC Morgan doesn't think so. She thinks the woman came down the corridor from the nurses' desk,' Jane replied. She continued, 'I'm also fairly sure that Mervin's death is somehow connected with the death of Rose Carter, though I don't know how. Meanwhile, we're dealing with a cold-blooded killer here, someone nasty enough to kill a sick man. And someone smart enough to get in and out of the hospital in the middle of the night without being noticed.'

As she finished speaking, a call came through from the hospital. Pete listened briefly and then told the team, 'They have no blonde women doctors on their staff at the moment.'

'I thought they might not, somehow,' Jane said. 'Right, let's brainstorm this.' She wrote on the board the names of all the people who had had any connection with the Rose Carter case. The detectives stared hopelessly at the list of people, wondering which of them had the opportunity, means, or motive, or whether, in fact, any of them had anything to do with Mervin's murder at all.

'Come on, then,' Jane urged her staff. 'What about possible motives?'

'Revenge?' DS Penny Kingdom suggested, a little wildly. 'For Rose's death?'

'Who did you have in mind, Penny?' Jane said.

'Well, I don't know. Jack Peck? We know Rose and he were lovers,' Penny replied.

'But would Jack kill his brother?' DC Tony Reilly asked.

'Well, it does seem rather unlikely,' Jane agreed. 'And anyway, as far as we know, the killer is female.'

'What about PAW? Perhaps one of them wanted revenge?' DC Maggie Pincombe suggested. 'That woman, Elisa Scott?'

'Well, I suppose that's just possible. They would certainly have the necessary skills to carry it out, from all accounts,' Jane replied. 'It could also have been done for no reason at all by an insane person, but the chances of that are very slim. I think the killer probably had very good reasons.' There was a long silence.

'OK,' Jane said finally. 'I want everyone to go through the paperwork, all the statements we've got, everything. Check and double check. Look for anything which might be worth following up.'

The team set to work with renewed enthusiasm. They had now had two mysterious deaths in just over a week, and compared to the usual business of trying to catch car thieves and burglars, this was exciting.

Jane went to her own office to do some thinking, getting a plastic mug of watery coffee from a machine on the way. Maybe Penny's suggestion had not been so fantastic: Jack Peck was certainly an odd character and sometimes extremes of emotion could lie hidden under the surface in people who disguised their feelings as he did. But was Jack Peck really so desperate that he would arrange the murder of his own brother? After all, he had visited the hospital at least twice, apparently concerned about his brother's welfare. On the other hand, he must have known roughly where Mervin was, which might possibly indicate his involvement in the crime.

A call came through from the pathologist. 'Would you like some early results of the postmortem on Mr Peck?' Dr Pat James enquired.

'Oh, hello, Pat. Find anything?' Jane said hopefully.

'Well, yes, as a matter of fact,' Pat James said. 'One cause of death was certainly suffocation, as they thought at the hospital.'

'What do you mean, one cause? Is there another cause? The infection on his arm?'

'Well, that was certainly very serious, but it had nothing to do with his death. No, but we did find a rather unusual substance in his blood, ketamine hydrochloride,' Pat James told her.

'What's that?'

'Ketamine hydrochloride is a powerful drug which is usually used by vets for animals, either as an anaesthetic or to kill them,' Pat James replied. 'If you wanted to murder someone, you could give them an injection of this stuff. If Mr Peck was asleep anyway, an injection wouldn't have woken him.'

'But why the suffocation?' Jane asked.

'Probably to make sure he really was dead.'

'Thanks, Pat, you've done a great job.' Jane put the phone down. Thoughts were buzzing round her head like flies. She went back into the CID office and stared at the list of names on the whiteboard.

'What's going on?' Pete asked, as he studied a display on

a computer screen. Jane repeated the information the pathologist had given her.

'Well,' he said thoughtfully, 'Hunter Products make animal vaccines, don't they? Perhaps they use animals in their research.'

'Of course! Pete, you're brilliant!' Jane gave him a broad smile. 'They might need to use a drug like ketamine hydrochloride in their research laboratories. So anyone who worked there would be able to get hold of some . . .'

'Such as Jo Keane,' Pete said.

'Or Jack Peck . . .' Jane suggested.

'Or even Susan Peck,' Pete finished her sentence just as the phone rang. It was Dr Fahid.

'What can I do for you, Dr Fahid?' Jane said.

'Ah, I thought that you may be interested to know that we have now got the results of Mr Peck's blood tests back from the laboratory,' the doctor said. 'You remember we sent them off last week when he first came in?'

'Yes I do. And?'

'Well, I was right,' Dr Fahid sounded pleased with himself. 'It seems that somehow Mr Peck had managed to get himself infected with *Clostridium septicam* and *Clostridium welchii*.'

'What do they mean?' asked Jane, almost apologetic that she didn't know these technical terms.

'Well, these are two of the bacteria which cause gas gangrene,' explained Dr Fahid. 'However, it's a little strange, an infection of this sort in a place like this. Normally gangrene is associated with war areas, you know, where people may have untreated wounds in very dirty places.'

'So how could he have picked it up?' Jane asked quietly. For some reason, as she had listened to him, his words had sent a chill down her spine. 'He hasn't been near a war, as far as I know.'

'We don't know,' Dr Fahid replied. 'It is quite mysterious. He has no other cuts or damage to his skin where the disease could have entered apart from his bee sting. So we have to assume it has something to do with that. On the other hand, although farms are not clean places, this seems a very unlikely explanation. So, to put it simply, I have absolutely no idea how he could have become infected.'

'Thanks, Dr Fahid,' Jane said and put the phone down thoughtfully.

'What's the matter?' asked Pete, who had been listening closely to this conversation. 'You look as if you've seen a ghost.'

'I don't know,' Jane answered slowly. 'Just something he said made me go quite cold. Pete, would you order me a car? I need to go out to Chittleham Farm again. I'd like you to keep an eye on things here. Someone needs to contact Mervin's lawyer and find out what he and Mervin talked about last Friday. And also go and see Elisa Scott at the PAW office. Ask her what she was doing on Saturday night.'

Chapter 15   *Something odd*

Out at Chittleham Farm the sun was shining on the yellow daffodils and other spring flowers that lined the lanes and fields. In the distance Jane could hear the familiar sound of sheep bleating, and nearby birds were singing with enthusiasm. Spring. She had never really seen spring so close up. You could almost feel everything growing, see the grass moving up towards the light, watch as the sticky brown buds on trees and hedges opened out into fresh green leaves. This astonishing sense of bursting out was quite unknown in the city. No wonder it was called 'spring' – it was such a sudden and large movement into life. It was breathtaking.

Inside Mervin Peck's farmhouse, nothing had changed since the last time Jane had been in there. She didn't know precisely what she was looking for, just that she would know it when she found it. She wandered from room to room, noticing yet again the faded fabrics, the mess and dirt. Upstairs it felt strange looking into Mervin's bedroom. The bed was unmade, the sheets piled in an untidy heap. It was almost as if he had only just got out of it.

In another room upstairs Jane spotted a large desk covered in papers. Mervin did not seem to have been a person who was organised about his personal affairs. There were bills, paid and unpaid, mixed up with letters on the open desk.

She had plenty of time. She went to the window and found that the room overlooked the lane where her driver, PC Dick Plumb, had parked the car.

'Dick,' she called out, opening the window. 'I'm going to be a while.'

'Right you are, ma'am,' he shouted back and settled down with his newspaper.

She closed the window again and set to work. After about half an hour, she had sorted the papers into categories. For no particular reason, she examined the letters first. There was nothing of any obvious interest: offers from insurance companies and building societies to take out savings plans. Next she looked through the bills, which were mainly for animal food, fence materials, car tyres, oil and petrol. No vets' bills, she noticed, surprising herself. She was beginning to think like a real countrywoman. If the man had sick animals, why didn't he call a vet in?

Finally, Jane looked at the bank statements. At first she noticed nothing. It was only on checking through a second time that she saw it: Mervin appeared to have £30,200 in his current account, which these days was a little odd. Most people put amounts of that size into savings accounts.

She studied the sheets carefully. They went back only two months but during that period there had been two payments of £6,000 into Mervin Peck's account. Perhaps there were more statements somewhere else? She tried a rusty old filing cabinet and was rewarded by a large brown envelope containing what looked like all Mervin's bank statements for the last five years.

She took the sheets of paper from the envelope and began to sort them into the correct order. It didn't take long to find out that during the previous October, November and December, Mervin had received three more payments of £6,000, making a total of £30,000. These were large payments for a struggling hill farmer. She would have to ask Mervin's bank for the source of these payments.

Suddenly Jane became aware of a loud, insistent buzzing sound, the kind made by a large flying insect. Looking around anxiously, she saw that a bee had somehow found its way into the room and was now trying to get out. In its desperation it threw itself against the glass of the closed window and then, turning, came flying towards her like a military jet on a bombing mission. Shivers went up and down her spine and the hair on the back of her neck stood up. Where on earth had the monstrous thing come from? She jumped sideways as the bee buzzed angrily past her head and turned to fly at her again. She gathered up the bank statements and ran from the room, shutting the door behind her with a bang. As she did so, she wondered why such small creatures always made her panic. Then she remembered Mervin's recent words about his brother's bees – 'Those bloody bees of his are dangerous!' – and felt less ashamed of herself.

Then it came to her in a flash. Why hadn't she seen it before? Bee stings. Both of the murder victims had been stung. Of course, it could just be a coincidence. But, equally, perhaps not.

'Seen a ghost, ma'am?' Dick Plumb cheerily remarked as she arrived breathless at the car. This was the second time today that someone had said this to her. She must look more tired than she realised.

'Yes, I think I just did,' she replied. 'Let's go. I've got what I came for. I think.'

Back at the office, Jane rang Mervin's bank and requested the source of the large payments. The woman at the bank said they would get back later in the day with the information. She put down the receiver and drummed her fingers on the desk. Why, in these hi-tech days of computers and electronics, couldn't they find the answer to a simple question quickly?

There was a knock at the door and Pete came in. Jane had by now given up trying to get him to wait for her permission to enter.

'We've been busy here, ma'am,' he announced grandly.

'I'm glad to hear it. Let's have it, then.'

'Right, well, the first thing is that when Mervin's lawyer saw him on Friday, Mervin asked the solicitor to give Jack a letter. He posted it through Jack's letter box on Friday night on his way home. He doesn't know what the letter said.

'The second thing is that we've got a few alibis confirmed. Elisa Scott stayed with a friend on Saturday night, and the friend confirmed, so she's off the suspect list. Jack and Susan Peck say they were both at home all the time, so either they were in it together, or neither of them was. Jack admits going to the hospital at about five o'clock on Saturday, however. Jo Keane says she was at a restaurant with friends on Saturday evening and got home around midnight. The restaurant has confirmed she was there.'

'Interesting,' Jane said thoughtfully. 'Listen, if you were

a farmer and you had a lot of very sick sheep, would you call in a vet?'

'Of course. You would have to. You can only treat relatively minor problems yourself. Most farmers have large vet's bills anyway. Animals get sick all the time. Why?' Pete looked puzzled.

'Hm . . .'

'What are you thinking about?' Pete asked again, just as the phone started to ring.

'Detective Chief Inspector Honeywell,' Jane said into the receiver. 'Yes? Oh . . . Really . . . Oh, I see. Right. Thanks very much. You've been very helpful. I wonder if you could put that in writing for me? Thanks a lot. Goodbye.'

Jane smiled with satisfaction. 'That was Mervin's bank,' she informed Pete. 'They have just confirmed that he received five payments of £6,000 from a company called Hunter Products Ltd. Not only that, but the arrangements were made by a Mr Jack Peck.'

'Wow!' Pete looked impressed, then frowned slightly. 'Yes, but so what?'

Jane laughed. 'I'm not sure exactly. But I think there's something very odd going on.'

'What do you mean?'

'I don't know. I don't know,' Jane answered. 'But it's something so important that people are being killed because of it.'

Pete's eyes widened. 'You mean it's not a simple case of a dark family secret, or a lover seeking revenge, that kind of thing?'

'No . . . I don't buy the revenge idea,' Jane found

herself saying. She hadn't realised she was so sure about that. 'No. I'm sure there's something else, much bigger, more serious . . .'

'You mean round here? In sleepy old Pilton?'

'Maybe,' Jane said. 'Anyway, we'd better pay another visit to Hunter Products, don't you think? Oh, by the way, who's looking after Mervin's sheep at the moment?'

'Old Mr Millman and the boy, as far as I know.'

'Well, could you ask the RSPCA to go up there? I can't imagine how the old man and his simple grandson can possibly manage to deal with all Mr Peck's animals on their own. I also think it might be safer for them if they didn't.'

Chapter 16   *Gotcha!*

Jane woke earlier than usual. She had had another wakeful night, her mind in a state of chaos and confusion. She knew that probably what she needed to know was there already; like looking for shells among stones on a beach, it was doubtless lying right under her nose.

The previous evening, for example, she had spent some time studying Rose Carter's diary again. Somewhere in it, she was positive, there must be something she had missed, something that might point to a connection between elements which had not until now seemed to be connected. Again she found the Thursday before Rose had died and stared at the entry:

JP – 3.00 !!!

Suddenly it struck her that the letters and numbers had been written in blue biro, but the exclamation marks were in heavy pencil, as if they had been added later. A tiny, subtle point, perhaps, but could it be significant? Anyway, why *had* Rose stopped her relationship with Jack, as Susan Peck had said? Jane wondered what sort of a person Rose was. What kind of woman would have an affair with Jack Peck, a married man, a man who seemed so cold and distant?

She had been once to Rose Carter's cottage. Maybe she should go back and take a closer look. She called the station to ask them to send a car round. Constable Dick

Plumb appeared soon after and they set off for South Heasley.

Rose Carter's house was typical of the area, a picture-postcard cottage with roses growing up the white walls and around the front door. In front, a well-cared-for garden was filled with a sea of plants. Looking at the pretty house with its dark windows and curtains drawn back, Jane fancied that it looked sad and lifeless somehow. It was odd how buildings could sometimes give off a sense that something unpleasant had happened to the people connected with them. A black cat appeared and wound itself round Jane's legs, miaowing with pleasure to see someone.

'Hello, puss. You're a friendly cat, aren't you?' Jane stroked the shiny black fur.

'He's missing his owner, I'm afraid.' A woman's voice came from behind Jane and she turned round.

'Does . . . did he belong to Miss Carter?' Jane asked.

'I'm afraid so, though we've been looking after him ever since . . . you know,' said the woman.

'I should introduce myself,' Jane said, showing her police identification. 'I've come to have a look round Miss Carter's house.'

'Pleased to meet you. I'll show you round, if you like. By the way, I'm Mary Brady.'

Inside the house it smelt stale and a little damp. The atmosphere was still: nothing had moved in there for a while to disturb the air, not since the SOCOs had been in a week ago. Nevertheless, Mary Brady seemed to take some pleasure in guiding Jane round the house. It seemed to be the house of an educated, intelligent woman. In the sitting room, which was painted a rich deep pink, crowded bookshelves covered three of the walls, and Chinese carpets in bright colours lay on the highly polished wooden floor. The well-designed kitchen contained a large square cooker typical of the houses in the region. The cooker was cold now but when warm it would have heated the whole house.

'It's a lovely house, isn't it? This was where she worked,' Mary Brady said, opening the door to a small room with more bookshelves, a workbench on one side and a desk against the opposite wall. There was a computer on the workbench, and next to it were some files neatly arranged and some boxes containing discs.

On top of the desk, which was piled high with notebooks and papers, Jane noticed a photograph and bent to study it. Rose – it must have been a young Rose – was smiling at the camera. Around her shoulders was the arm of her companion, a tall serious-looking man: Jack Peck, also much younger. Perhaps Jack hadn't always been such a cold fish?

Turning to Mary Brady, Jane said, 'Has anyone been here that you know of since Rose died?'

'You mean apart from the police? Well, as it happens, that man came a day or two ago. Yes, Sunday.' She pointed to the photo on the desk. 'He used to visit her a lot, as I told your colleagues the other day. I said hello to him and he said he had to collect something of his from Rose's house. He was quite quick so he must've got what he wanted.'

'Look,' Jane said, 'I'm going to have to check the files on Rose's computer so I may be a few minutes.'

'Oh, fine. I'll leave you in peace, then,' Mary Brady replied and went back to her garden.

Jane switched on the computer and stared at the list of files displayed on the screen. There was nothing that seemed worth looking at. Had Jack come to collect Rose's unfinished work? If so, where was it? She remembered an old detective's trick: always check dustbins. Quickly she found the 'recycle bin' where deleted files were stored. Listed there were two files called *HP\Samson.xls* and *HP\RiftValley.xls*. Something about the words in the filenames struck her as familiar, though she could not for the moment think why. *HP*, though, surely that must stand for Hunter Products? They had been deleted two days before.

She tried *RiftValley*.

'Gotcha!' she exclaimed.

HP\RiftValley turned out to contain pages and pages of numbers and mathematical signs, and nothing else. She tried *HP\Samson* and found a similar set of data. Taking a clean floppy disc, she copied both the files and put the disc in her bag, grinning to herself. If Jack Peck had been trying to destroy those two files, he had not done it properly.

She shut down the computer, went out of the house and found Mary Brady attending to her plants in her garden.

'Thanks for showing me the house,' Jane said. 'I'll be off now.'

'Not at all,' Mary Brady said. 'I do hope the person who did this awful thing to Rose goes to prison for a long time. She was much loved around here, you know. We were all so shocked to hear about it.'

As Jane sat in the car on the way back to Pilton, she remembered where she had seen the word Samson before.

In Rose's diary, written a week before she had seen Jack Peck for the last time, had been the words:

What exactly is Samson? Ask J

How strange. Could it be that Rose didn't really know what it was she was working on for Hunter Products?

And what about Rift Valley? Why was that name familiar? She thought hard for a bit and finally gave up. It would come to her later.

Then something Pete had said last night started floating around in her mind.

As soon as she arrived in her office, Jane dialled the number for PAW. 'DCI Honeywell here. Is that Elisa Scott?' she said to the friendly, familiar voice on the other end.

'Yes, it's Elisa here. How can I help? Any more car chases?' Elisa laughed softly.

'No, sorry to disappoint you!' Jane grinned into the phone. 'But can you tell me exactly what happened when Rose came in to the PAW office the Friday before she died?'

'Sure. She just came in and told me she was going to go out to Chittleham Farm again in the next few days.'

'Did she say why?' Jane asked.

'Just that she was quite concerned about the animals there.'

'Nothing else?'

'No, although she did seem a bit depressed, when I think about it,' Elisa said thoughtfully.

'Thanks, Elisa,' Jane said. 'That's very helpful.'

'Is it?' Elisa sounded surprised. 'I hope so. You know I got the RSPCA out to look at those sheep. They were in a terrible . . .'

'Yes,' said Jane vaguely, thinking about the pieces of the puzzle that now seemed to be falling into place. 'That's great . . .' She said goodbye and hung up.

What had really been going on at Chittleham Farm? There must have been something odd. Why else would Mervin have been paid those large amounts of money by Hunter Products? Jane wondered how much Rose had known.

Rose must have broken off her relationship with Jack on the Thursday before she died. Had they had an argument of some sort? Was that why she had added those exclamation marks to her diary entry? Perhaps it had gone like this: she had wanted to know what Samson meant; and then she had asked the question whose answer she dreaded but which she probably already knew: did Hunter Products test their products on animals?

If the answer had been positive, how torn she would have felt: she was involved with the animal rights protesters' movement while simultaneously not only working for a company that used animals in their research, but also having an affair with one of its employees.

Rose had been planning to go back to Chittleham Farm anyway, to check the animals again. Did she know that it belonged to Jack's brother? Perhaps the animals at Chittleham Farm were somehow involved in Jack's company's work. Had Rose put two and two together last Thursday and made four?

Chapter 17 *The bee*

At Hunter Products, the receptionist welcomed Jane and Pete with her usual humourless expression. She would try to get Mrs Keane but as far as she knew Mrs Keane was busy all day. Jane had to lean on the counter and bark an order so that the receptionist jumped slightly and did as she was asked.

'What a cheerful, helpful person she is!' Pete remarked.

'Isn't she?' Jane agreed. The receptionist stared at them furiously. After a few moments, Jo Keane arrived through the door into the reception area. Today the elegant business suit was an eggshell blue, matching the arctic eyes.

'What can I do for you?' she enquired politely.

'Well, we'd like to have a look around the factory, if you don't mind,' Jane informed her.

A curious expression moved rapidly across Jo Keane's perfectly made-up face, and there was a brief pause. 'I'm afraid that's out of the question,' she announced finally. 'Visitors are not allowed into the factory area for health reasons. We have to maintain the strictest standards of cleanliness or we would lose our licence. Unless, of course, you have a search warrant?' The ice-blue eyes seemed to harden as they met Jane's and the words contained an unmistakable challenge.

After the smallest hesitation, Jane said, 'You produce animal vaccines here, don't you?'

'That's correct,' Jo Keane replied.

'I suppose then you must carry out experiments on animals?'

'Yes, that's true,' Jo Keane said. 'In fact, that's the reason why we have such tight security. Other companies similar to ours have had a lot of trouble with animal rights protesters. We don't want anyone to break in and free all the animals – the mice, rabbits and so on. It would be disastrous.'

'Oh well, no, of course. You can't be too careful, can you?' Pete commented cheerfully.

'Would it be possible to have a quick word with Jack Peck before we leave?' Jane asked.

'I'm terribly sorry, but he's out of the office at the moment. He'll be in tomorrow, if you'd like to call back?'

'Not to worry, then, we'll try again,' Jane said. 'Might I just use the ladies' on my way out?'

'Of course,' Jo Keane said and showed her where to go.

Inside the ladies' toilet, like everywhere else in the factory, it was spotlessly clean. Jane glanced up at the security camera fixed high up in one corner. As she did so, she suddenly noticed a bee crawling sleepily up the wall. For the second time in twenty-four hours the hair on the back of her neck felt electric and she had to work to control her fear. Why did there seem to be bees everywhere she went?

Looking up again at the camera which had moved its watchful stare across to the other side of the room, Jane quickly found a handkerchief and trapped the bee inside it. It buzzed pathetically, too sleepy to protest much as she placed it carefully inside her bag. She would send the bee off to one of the Government's forensic laboratories, together with the floppy discs from Rose's cottage. Perhaps someone would be able to make sense of it all. The camera was beginning to swing back again towards Jane. Quickly she looked in the mirror, made as if to adjust her hair and then left the room.

Outside, Pete said, 'Well, that wasn't very productive, was it?'

'No, it wasn't. We really need to get inside that factory and see what they're up to. We're going to have to get a warrant, but I'm not sure there's time now . . .' Jane paused. 'Anyway, look what I found in the ladies' loo.' She showed Pete her handkerchief from inside which a weak buzzing sound was coming.

'What on earth . . . ?' Pete began.

'I've no idea,' Jane said.

Back at the station Jane shut herself in her office. She needed to make a phone call in private.

'Hello, Elisa, Jane here again,' she said. 'I'm hoping you'll be able to help me with another little job. *Tonight.*' When she told Elisa what she had in mind, there was a long silence. But as Jane had guessed, Elisa was more than willing to help out.

No sooner had she put the phone down than another call came through. It was Susan Peck, wanting to talk to her confidentially. Jane arranged a meeting in a pub not far from Susan's house for that evening, and didn't get back to her flat until after ten. As soon as she opened the door the phone rang. It was Pete.

'Guess what, ma'am!' he announced. 'There's been an animal rights break-in at Hunter Products. They somehow got through the security system, tied up the night watchman and let out all the animals.'

'Did they really? Good heavens,' Jane said.

'Yes,' Pete went on. 'We had an anonymous phone call . . .' There was a pause. Then he stammered, 'You d . . d . . didn't . . . ?'

'Didn't what?' Jane asked. 'Didn't what?'

'Oh . . . er . . . nothing.'

'It's time we got Operation Wasp going, isn't it? All these break-ins . . .' There was a noticeable groan at the other end of the line. 'Come and pick me up in about ten minutes, will you?' Jane told him.

Outside the south-west wind had stopped blowing for once, and the clear night sky was as black as coal and dotted with silvery stars, as Jane and Pete set off for Hunter Products.

'Life has not exactly been quiet since you arrived down here, has it, ma'am?' Pete remarked. 'Two murders inside a week, and now a major break-in here. I suppose it's just a coincidence?' The question hung in the air.

Jane smiled. 'It's good to keep busy, don't you think? Come on, let's go in and see what this place is all about,' said Jane, thinking that at last they were able to look around the inside of the factory.

The first room they tried was full of TVs, wires, video recorders, red and green flashing lights. Pete gave a low whistle. The equipment was the best that money could buy for the purpose of spying on visitors, factory employees and their activities, anything and everything inside and outside the building.

Jane and Pete stood in front of the bank of screens and

stared in silence. In some of the rooms the pictures showed what looked like large metal containers – similar to those used for making beer, as Pete said afterwards – connected to each other by a network of large pipes. In one or two of the rooms, boxes that looked like small animal cages were piled from floor to ceiling, though it was impossible to see what was inside them.

They left the security control room and found themselves next in the animal vaccine research section where the rooms were filled with microscopes, bottles, white gloves and other pieces of equipment. Jane examined the lines of bottles carefully. After a few minutes her eyes fell on a large bottle labelled: 'Ketalar – contents: ketamine hydrochloride'.

'Go and tell the SOCOs to check this for fingerprints, would you?' she told Pete.

Looking further round the room, she saw a filing cabinet and rapidly opened the drawers. She was in luck. At the front of one of the drawers there was a file named Samson. She pulled out the file and glanced though the papers. Among them was a letter from an African Colonel. It read:

We look forward to receiving the Samson supplies in the next month. $1 million has been paid into your account in Switzerland as agreed. The balance is to be paid on receipt of the goods.

Jane put the letter in her pocket.

Suddenly she became aware of a soft movement behind her and almost screamed when she turned round: the room was full of creatures – rabbits, mice and rats, jumping and running around, exploring their new-found freedom. Behind the animals, Pete was grinning in the doorway.

'Where the hell did they come from?' Jane yelled.

'Animal liberation,' said Pete laughing. 'The SOCOs are still trying to round them all up, poor things. Come and see what I've found.'

Jane followed him down to a room they had seen on the security cameras – the one lined with small cages. Jane peered into a cage from which an odd buzzing sound seemed to be coming.

'Mosquitoes?' she queried.

'I reckon so,' Pete replied, in his dreadful Texan accent, which Jane tried unsuccessfully to ignore.

Then she remembered – Rift Valley. That had been the name of that virus disease on the TV the other night. The one carried by mosquitoes. In a strange kind of slow motion, the true nature of the work being done at Hunter Products began to dawn on her, and she realised with sickening horror that she needed to act very fast.

Chapter 18 *Operation Wasp*

'OK, Pete,' Jane said urgently. 'Listen very carefully. It's vitally important that we get this right. I don't have time to explain right now. You'll just have to trust me. I'll explain on the way back to the station.' Pete looked at her in surprise, impressed by the sudden note of seriousness in her voice.

'Yes, ma'am,' he said, dropping his Texan accent now, as they walked back to the car.

'First, the factory has to be sealed off. No-one, repeat no-one, is to be allowed in. We need to set up road blocks on all the roads out of Pilton. What we have to do is find Jo Keane and Jack Peck, before they have a chance to leave Pilton. We can get Operation Wasp up and running right now, with whatever staff we've got available. You arrange that. Then I want you to go to Jack Peck's house and, if he's there, arrest him.'

'What for?' Pete asked, his eyes wide with astonishment.

'The murder of his brother,' Jane replied, matter of factly.

'But . . . I thought it was supposed to be a woman who did it?'

'It was, in a way.'

'But why? What's it all about?'

'Can't go into it now,' Jane said. 'I'll tell you later. Anyway, I also want you to send someone round to Jo

Keane's house to bring her in as well. We'll just have to hope that they haven't decided to disappear already.'

'But wouldn't they want to come here, to look at the damage to their factory?' Pete asked.

'Well, if I'm right, they won't bother. They'll want to get right away as fast as they possibly can,' Jane replied.

As soon as they arrived back at Pilton Police Station, Jane placed an urgent call to MI6 in London. She had just finished when Pete came back to say that he had set up some road blocks, and that he was now going to pick up Jack Peck. Tony Reilly and Maggie were going to get Jo Keane.

A few moments after Pete had disappeared, a police constable on duty at the factory rang. Oh no, now what? Jane asked herself pessimistically. What could have gone wrong so quickly? The constable informed her that two people, a man and a woman, had arrived and demanded to go inside. He had told them no-one was to be allowed into the factory and they had become rather angry.

'What did they do?' Jane asked him. 'Have they gone?'

'Yes, ma'am. They went off in something of a hurry.'

'Did you get the car registration?'

'Yes, ma'am. An MG sports car, P registration.'

'Good lad,' Jane told him. She went quickly to the radio room to send out an order to all the road blocks to stop the MG if it appeared and arrest the occupants on sight. No sooner had she had finished than another message came in.

'PC Dick Plumb speaking, ma'am. I'm on the South Heasley road out of Pilton. I'm afraid we've got a slightly awkward situation here.' PC Plumb's voice sounded nervous.

'What situation, Dick?'

'Er . . . well, we stopped a man who then pulled out a gun. He's taken WPC Morgan, the new officer. He says he's going to shoot her if we don't let him through. I presume it's Mr Peck.'

'OK, I'm on my way. Try and keep him talking will you? Whatever happens, don't let him drive off, you hear?'

She picked up the microphone to send out another message instructing all the road block units to head for the South Heasley road. Then, having phoned Pete, Tony and Maggie and told them to cover the road from South Heasley to Buxton, she ran down to the garage, found a car and drove as fast as she could out to where PC Plumb and WPC Morgan had been stationed.

Arriving at the road block, halfway between South Heasley and Pilton, Jane was horrified to see, in the lights of her car, that PC Plumb was sitting on the ground, leaning against his car, holding his head. Blood seemed to be pouring down his face.

'Dick,' Jane shouted from her open window. 'Where are they? Are you all right?'

'I'm OK, ma'am. It's just a surface wound. But he's got WPC Morgan, ma'am. Mr Peck dragged her into his car and attacked me when I tried to stop him. They've gone off that way.' Dick Plumb pointed towards South Heasley. In the dark, Jane made out the glow of car headlights moving towards the sleeping village of South Heasley. She might just be able to catch them.

The powerful police Volvo roared along the country road, its siren screaming. Somehow Jane did not care about anything that might be in her path. The only thought in her head was to reach the disappearing MG. As the lights of the village drew nearer, she thought she was gaining ground. She remembered that the village streets were extremely narrow coming in from this side and there was a tight corner just before the village square. Jack Peck would have to slow down through the village.

She called Pete on her mobile phone. 'Pete, where are you? Jack Peck's making a run for it. He's got WPC Morgan.'

'I'm between Buxton and South Heasley.' Pete's voice sounded faint in the speaker.

'OK, I can see the tail lights now. I'm catching them up. He knows I'm after him and he's going much too fast through the village. Oh my God, he's just braked . . .' Jane broke off as she could see the MG begin to slide. It came to a sudden stop, crashing against a stone wall.

'Pete, get here as fast as you can. And turn your siren off.'

Around the square in the middle of South Heasley lights came on in several upstairs windows and astonished faces of villagers appeared, staring at the scene below them. In the dim glow of the streetlights, Jane noticed a small black shape lying still on the ground near Jack Peck's car. A cat. He must have hit a cat. She hoped, irrelevantly, that it was not Rose's cat.

As she moved cautiously towards the MG, the door opened and Jack got out, holding a gun pointed at someone inside the car. Then WPC Morgan climbed out.

Jack grabbed her and, holding her in front of him with his hand over her mouth, shouted, 'She gets it if you come any closer!'

'OK, I'll stop here,' Jane said. 'Where's Jo?'

'I don't know. I don't care,' he said desperately. 'I need your car. You let me go or I'll shoot this young lady here.'

Jane could see that WPC Morgan was rigid with fear and near to collapse, but Jane needed to play for time.

'All right, Mr Peck. You win. But before I make the call, just tell me this, why did you murder your own brother?'

'Move away from your car,' Jack Peck screamed. Jane moved away from her car. Peck approached holding the young WPC in front of him.

'Adopted brother,' he corrected her, as if this somehow made it better. 'Mervin was a fool anyway.'

'OK, but why kill him?' Jane insisted. Jack adjusted his hold on WPC Morgan. He was beginning to get nervous now.

'Mervin sent me a letter from hospital . . . He was threatening to tell the authorities what had been going on at his farm unless I did something to get him out of the mess he was in.'

'Did Jo tell you to do it?'

'No. No-one tells me what to do.' Jack Peck sounded annoyed. 'We did it together . . .' Jack was beside the police car now.

'Together? I had a feeling Jo was the "blonde doctor".' Jack Peck didn't answer.

'Aren't you lovers?' asked Jane to stall for time. 'You and Ms Keane?' Just then she saw a movement on the other side of the square behind Jack. It was Pete, edging quietly closer.

Jack Peck walked around the car and saw the keys weren't in the ignition.

'Where are the keys?' he screamed.

'Answer my question first.'

'We were, once upon a time. Now, no, just business partners. Now, the keys!'

'What kind of business is it, Mr Peck, which means that two people, Rose and your brother, have to die?'

'Chief Inspector Honeywell, you're not stupid. If you stood to make several million dollars, you'd do the same.'

'OK, maybe I would,' Jane said. A few more seconds and Pete would be close enough. 'So that's why the sheep were sick, then, because you were testing out the Rift Valley virus on them?'

'You're smart, Chief Inspector, I'll give you that. Now, would you give me those keys please?' he said in a low voice, the gun still pointed at WPC Morgan's head.

Keep going, keep going, Jane told herself. She held up the keys. 'So Mervin was in it too, then?' she continued.

'No. He didn't know what it was we were really doing, he was just supposed to keep visitors away. He did it for the money. Unfortunately, he always had a terrible temper.'

'So what was the Samson project?'

'We'd perfected a way of using bees to deliver stings that go gangrenous,' Jack Peck said. He added proudly, 'It was my own invention.'

Then everything happened at once. Jane threw the keys on the ground in front of Jack and Jack turned the gun away from WPC Morgan for a split second, which gave Pete Fish enough time to make his move. He came up rapidly behind Jack, grabbed his arms and held them up behind his back. The gun fell from his hands and, as it hit the ground, a bullet was fired harmlessly into the air. Jack uttered a cry of anger and frustration.

'Jack Peck, you are under arrest,' Jane announced, going quickly up to him and putting a pair of handcuffs on him. 'You don't have to say anything, but it may harm your defence if . . .'

As she finished reading him his rights, Tony Reilly and Maggie Pincombe drove up in a police car with Jo Keane in the back seat.

'We found her driving out of town with her bags packed and a plane ticket to Argentina,' said Tony Reilly.

'Well,' said Jane, grinning with satisfaction. 'Operation Wasp has stung.'

Chapter 19   *Astonishing evil*

It was one of those magical days people imagine when they think of springtime, one of those days which people wait for all winter. Only good things can happen on days like this, Jane thought, as she stood outside Hunter Products. The sun was rising into a clear blue sky, promising a day so sunny and warm that the early morning mist would soon lift like steam off the fields. In the beauty of the early morning all human cruelty and horror and evil seemed somehow impossible, just a stupid joke, a bad dream.

Chief Superintendent George Ferguson was standing beside her, having just arrived. They were watching several men in white suits – an Army special unit from London – removing the contents of the Hunter Products factory and putting them into white vans.

'I didn't like to wake you up last night to explain. See those boxes?' Jane said to George, with a slightly secretive air. 'They're insect cages, with mosquitoes in them.'

'So?'

'You ever heard of Ebola Fever? Rift Valley Fever?'

'No,' George said. 'What on earth are you talking about?'

'By pure coincidence,' Jane answered, 'I saw something about them on TV the other night. They're especially unpleasant viruses which have caused epidemics in Africa. Last night, when we were called out to the break-in here

. . . well, I suddenly realised what Hunter Products were up to. I contacted MI6 in London and they said they had been watching this company for some time. Until now they've had no firm evidence to go on.'

'So what *are* they up to?' George asked, looking extremely confused.

'Well, although Hunter Products do make agricultural chemicals and animal vaccines, that's just a cover. Their main business is biological warfare and, in particular, the use of insects as carriers of deadly diseases. What's more, they were about to export their products illegally to a country which has a rather violent ruler in control. Anyway, MI6 will now have all the proof they need.'

'I suppose,' George said, 'that none of this is to be made public?'

'MI6 would like it to remain top secret, yes. The general public cannot possibly be allowed to get the slightest whisper of what this company was doing. Anyway, it's more than likely that no-one except the managing director and the scientific director – Jo Keane and Jack Peck, that is – knew what the company really did. The other employees probably thought they were making vaccines.'

'Jane, I'm proud of you,' George said.

'If you'll excuse me sir, I've got a murder case to wrap up.' She smiled. 'We need to ensure that the people in charge of this business go to prison for a long while.'

*   *   *

'Well, come on then, ma'am,' Pete said after Jane and he had interviewed Jack Peck and Jo Keane and then charged them with murder and conspiracy. 'However did you work

109

it all out? How did you know it was Jack that murdered Mervin? Female intuition?'

'No, Pete,' Jane replied with gentle irony in her voice. 'It was actually something you said the other night. About either Jack and Susan Peck both being in it together or not at all. I realised that there could have been two people at the hospital. WPC Morgan was attacked from behind, so someone else could have come from out of the service lift while the so-called doctor kept her occupied.

'Then I saw Susan Peck last night. It seems Jack had made her promise not to tell anyone that he was out of the house until well after midnight on Saturday night. She didn't know what he'd been doing, but when he came in she noticed that he smelt. He probably just smelt of some chemical, but she was convinced he'd been with another woman. She wasn't going to provide him with an alibi just so he could be with someone else. That, she told me, was mad. She withdrew the alibi and she's going to divorce him. She's had enough.'

'I feel sorry for that woman,' Pete remarked.

'She wasn't the only one to suffer,' Jane pointed out. 'He seems to have had no conscience at all. He exploited Rose Carter quite heartlessly, and Mervin became an unknowing guinea pig for his evil experiments.'

'There's something I don't understand,' Pete said. 'Jack must have known about Rose's interest in animal rights. Wasn't it rather dangerous to involve her in his research?'

'You're right,' Jane replied. 'He admitted it was a stupid mistake. He and Rose knew each other from college days, so he helped her out a bit when she first moved here by giving her some work. After a while they started to have an affair and then when they needed someone to do the statistical work on *Rift Valley*, someone outside the factory, he gave it to her. He thought she would just accept it if he told her that they weren't using animals for experiments. Rose seems to have trusted him for a while. Apparently, she believed he was developing vaccines for diseases in Africa.

'Then on the Thursday before she died, she got him to admit that he did test some of his products on animals. They had a big argument about it and she said she wanted nothing more to do with him. Anyway, she must have guessed that some of the experimental animals were kept at Chittleham Farm.'

The team listened in shocked silence. Despite her delight at the successful outcome, Jane now began to feel sickened. Sometimes her work revealed aspects of human nature that she found hard to cope with. People were capable of astonishing evil. Surprisingly, this had turned out to be as true in this sleepy country place, where families brought their children for holidays, where people came to escape the pressures of big city life, as it was in a city environment. She had to remind herself that the work she did helped to uncover some of the bad things and prevent more of them occurring.

'Pete,' she said, standing up, 'I'm going home. I've been up all night. I'm exhausted.'

'I'll drive you, shall I?' he asked.

'Yes, please,' she answered.

Sitting in Pete's car outside her flat, she suddenly did not want to be alone just now. She needed company, human company. Julian the cat was not sufficient. And she felt like cooking.

111

She took a coin out of her bag and threw it up in the air.

'What are you doing?' Pete asked as she covered the coin with her hand. Heads, she would ask him, tails she wouldn't. She uncovered the coin. It was heads.

'Do you fancy a curry?' she said.